T0128491

PSST!
HOMIE!

A NOVEL

ALEX GARCIA

authorHOUSE®

AuthorHouse™
1663 Liberty Drive
Bloomington, IN 47403
www.authorhouse.com
Phone: 1 (800) 839-8640

Published by AuthorHouse 04/24/2020

ISBN: 978-1-7283-5989-2 (sc)
ISBN: 978-1-7283-5988-5 (e)

Library of Congress Control Number: 2020907375

To our wonderful administration
at Centinela Valley Adult
School at Lawndale, Califas. My heartfelt homies.

CONTENTS

IN THE BEGINNING

Homie *n, (hō-mee)*: a contemporary slang term for dude, bro or homeboy, a friend or *nigga-please*. A 1990's popular hip-hop group, Lighter Shade of Brown, defined it in their song title "Homies" as, "Little traviesos [rascals] that are always into doing something bad acting like they did nothing." This lucid memoir is part knowledge, part exam, and delving into our ever-changing penitentiary mechanism. Precisely, a cage's steely bars and its captive. As famed anthropologist Thomas Henry Huxley teaches, "It is important to remember that, in strictness, there is no such thing as an uneducated man." *(A Liberal Education)*

And there was light.

We will begin our discovery journey at a Los Diablos County Youth Hall, then onto an unexpected merge of miscellaneous cultures in Twin Titans Corrective Facilities' underworld. Afterward, a two-year prison sentence inside of Califa's Rehab Rangers countered by a brief stint in Immigration and Naturalization's Clearway Correctional Authorities. Its aftermath, a furtive deportation to Honduras, Central America, and yet one final arrest that encircled an allusive lesson.

They say that life is routine and needs a getting used to,

for example, learning to walk, jog, sleep and to ride a bicycle. However, to get used to *jail*? If so, what are *key* ingredients to survive in danger-filled maximum-security territories?

This is my biography that sprung almost thirty years of recidivism through various corrective centers and although this narrative is antique, no one denies that prison text does not get old, people do. Furthermore, these testy exploits happen continuously and unexpectedly to average citizens in countries throughout our planet. Prisons will never become extinct; they only increase in numbers and harshness. Are our old maxims "once in jail—always in jail; or, some people just never learn," *true*?

Prayerfully, be my guest; read on; enter.

OUR HOMIE

Our homeboy knows...

Lil Homie-don't-you-know-me, this is a brief holler at yah from your forty-six-year-old uncle on a relaxed summer sunset. What is going on with you inside of that county jail? Cool, calm, and collecting *stripes*— gracious ones, hopefully. It has been over seven years from our last hug. I have been gone from our family for a good chunk of time but that is how humankind evolves inside and outside of our imaginary murals. Inspirit, right now, it is not so much about me— because I am reclined in my bedroom drinking a few beers, reminiscing at a portrait of our disassociated family that includes you at five years of age. Within this photograph, clearly visible is that it took significance in a front porch of an old Clayborne Elementary Faculty, Zeon Davis; our graduate wore a white gown and mortarboard cap.

A second colorful and jubilant picture is of your mother, your younger siblings, and you, lively embraced. At that moment you had just turned sixteen years young as we celebrated your birthday while we took advantage of our free Family Night tickets we had won on a raffle to sit at Chavas Chasm's upper-deck last empty row to enjoy a miles' off miniature baseball game without binoculars—*Go Badgers!*

Anyhow, your mom and I have not spoken in more than a year; however, our latest family rumor is that she stays in the Harbour Area with your two younger sisters. She drives, although a few miles at a time, in a discolored faulty Honda Civic with its muffler exploding black smoke clouds at every ignition and intersections - *but it beats the can!* Luckily, she has not received any costly tickets for accrued junkyard property, smog-check failures, expired tags or reckless driving for its wobbly hind rims, fake loose seat belts and broken taillights. Besides, little homie, I need not worry you any further as you can j-u-s-t imagine its overall rusted metal carcass that resembles Los Diablos' Wyatts Towers—*remember?* Her wheeled Noah's Arc has four slippery tires that look like watermelons and a weak creaking undercarriage with our family's heftiness dismantling it even more; you know how we do it. On a positive angle, *one key note*, and that is that once this embarrassed casket falls apart, our food stamps cannot purchase even a pull-push go-kart. Let us thank our resplendent angels and legislators for social assistance.

Your ecclesiastical aunt prays for your blessings as she keeps in touch with your cousins, who live in Virginia, maybe four times a year via telephone and internet and they said "Hi, and to take care," "—of your soap!" they joked. So, where are you keeping healthy? That is, I still do my twenty sit-ups, fifteen pushups, and two or three full pull-ups every now and then, here and there, yet a practical relief is a daily Yoga practice to hold a serene soul. A major maintenance component to aid one self's liveliness and wholesomeness is to concentrate, inside or outside of our mesh pit.

November 6, 2016 as year-end festivities are near, happy

holidays. My sincere wish is for this *kite* to reach you before new-years-day—and have a letter to feel cheer! A quick response from you will be marvelous and appreciated as I cross my fingers, God-first.

Okay holmes, as famous rapper 2-Pac sings, "Keep Ya Head Up." Life withers, my bedtime has arrived as a radiant day awaits, and as this proverb goes, our sun always shines brighter outside. Everyone in Honduras, Central America.

Good luck lil homie.

BOYS, INTERRUPTED

Some of us congregate and stand or sit in front of an old-fashioned casket-like blurry television clamped in a corner of our enclosed empty dayroom to catch our evening news, awestruck, a lone sharp derisive juvenile delinquent warns, "Darn-diddy-d-a-yemm! Iz a crazy world out-there. I showw-ammh glad I'm in here." A few more kids stand nearby; they gesture and laugh at invisible objects or persons.

A sub-city in an immense sandy dune: a canteen, medical clinic, laundry, a commissary and dining hall. Annexed to it is a sports and fitness gym, heck, even an isolated jail that we tagged the SHU Box, Solitary Housing Unit. Not that we are exempt from real-time outside decisions and responsibilities; a contrary expectancy progresses. We must search and acquire a job, be on time to do our duty, rarely *see* a doctor, maintain a decent hygiene schedule or attend a trade shop to undertake a technical trade.

In this remote area, one cannot relent to supernatural catastrophes such as mild earthquakes, dust tornadoes, thunderstorms and ferocious fires. We manage these phenomena with a handy fist-of-its-kind First-Aid kit as its tweezer, thermometer and surgical utensils are digital. *Good gracious* that some of us are technology savvy. We duplicate outside society with violence and deadly boxing duels; however, we are uncritical of any media hype in search of a Mafioso in a thrilled *whodunit Owe-Jay* syndrome or superfluous forensic investigative follow-ups.

Undeniably, we need not necessarily be insane to intercept ourselves in a psychiatric ward, blind to ignore, guilty of a crime to sit in a prison cell or be physically dead to feel and considered as such. In here, we are on our own, same as in their real free divisions. Congrats! We made it. Welcome.

LIL HOMIES; BIG WOUNDS

The family, or as Latin actors lusciously say in films, *la familia*. At six this morning, off to the big homies Academy's Resource Center—which is routine, to study in there every Saturday from seven until lights-out at noon. Its resource center is superbly quiet as our aged homie is usually alone with a couple librarians and their full service on subject matters and, in turn, they are utmost helpful.

At one p.m., already at home and awaiting a soccer match to start on their giant screen television when an unsuspected sluggishness lassoed his body, therefore, took a nap and woke up close to four o'clock and missed his event. Nevertheless, coming up at five is one more sought-after game that promises to be of interest so his meantime plan is to ride a bicycle to a nearby track and jog for about an hour. However, as he left, a nine-year-old girl entered his house in wild screams and panted so he asked her, why are you crying? Her hands trembled as she pointed to her twin brother of ten years of age who trailed.

This kid stopped his fright at the door as he sobbed and held a wrapped chunk of ice on his inflated face so his big homie asked about it. He did not answer. Hastily, out of nowhere, a neighborly child butted in, said that his dad was angry, and punched him. Blood boiled as their old homies' anger overpassed and blanketed logic and reason as he rushed to their backyard to inquire about what really occurred and, as always, found their same druggie involved in their latest intense domestic dispute with his go-to wife, and as a result, pounded their young homie's face.

La familia, discussed angrily again as they threw brooms, mops, and gardening tools around amidst their barbecue area and yelled across themselves—as everyone was eager to get close to their scumbag to get a wad of him. Amidst their turmoil, a neighbor dialed 9-1-1, causing on their perpetrator a cause to escape and this thought increased their desperate attempt to reconcile especially to save the sobbing kid from foster care. Within their commotions, a group of neighbors had quickly gathered and stood next to their gate as their creep started to run as he tried tackling maneuvers to get away from them but they mobbed his arms and held him tight until the cops arrived or else he would flee. Somehow, they calmed, their chaos under control, everyone taking a deep breath, and their thug broke free.

Now, one of our little homies' family members gave chase and pulled their runaway creep by the back of his shirt collar as hatred and violence resurged like a boil of lava. "Shut up!" They screamed at him as they held him and listened for just one more expletive to use as an excuse to rush him full-fisted. It seemed like an overdue beating to serve their two Akitas recompense for his nightly punts at these dogs for no reason whatsoever.

Amidst discord, he became loose and staggered toward the exit, madly staring at everyone and hollering a lot of boloney but still swung airy punches at everyone. People exchanged uppercuts, jabs and wild midair fisted swings and wanna-be karate kicks—and some of those raged hits were precise. Undeniably, this incident provoked an outrage thus his deserved whooping for this defenseless child's trounce—and for a galore of drunken profanities he had needlessly unleashed and bullied on most of his family members.

As their battle unfolded with every ones' tempers and logics interchanged rhythms but still out of an outcry for everyone witnessed this kid's red face as it steadily swelled. Out of nowhere, an older man broke into their intense bickering and to separate everyone as he started to repeat, "Ya'll don't have to bring this problem this far." *Dude! Nonsense.* This victimizer needs a serious lesson and more so as he will soon head to jail—so their least bit of empathy as a last opportunity to send him crippled on his way. A pummeling that will not be for themselves uniquely but beyond this incident, payback for all previous party disasters.

This goon screwed their family's weekend cookout by forcibly, and dishonorably, humiliated a ten-year-old child as he knocked him to the driveway, unapologetic. Thus, somewhere, a jail cell awaits him, anywhere, to rot. In spite of that, with our doubtful judicature and its broad loopholes, any kind of surprised verdict may occur.

Yet this subjective, emotional and physical traumatization of this generation has transpired for many years—just as it happens in some families—and our poverty combined with alcohol is, perhaps, why these same incidents are repetitive and without family sympathy. The old man who broke in said that if it had been our little homie's twin sister then he would have gotten involved physically too—but it was not her. *Dude!* This crook knocked down a defenseless soul with one manly barbaric blow. Moreover, he possesses beastly strength as it measured Richter scale degrees when they exchanged facial punches and solid enough to knock anyone down as they broke their backyard fence with their forces' intensity when they became hooked on it.

Just last week, for instance, one midday, while he organized their messy garage and some girls enjoyed a jumpy hammock in their backyard when, with sudden suspense, this same neighborly villain started to hatefully bellow vulgarities at his daughter as his fury increased while he uttered continuous obscenities at his innocent playful girl. Tears filled her eyes as she quivered incessantly. What can she do? What can they do? What can we do when he does not listen to sound advice? He refers to her as *his little girl*.

Now, with their declined deceptions, the cops took their explosive harasser to jail as their child had a purple cheekbone that protruded and a bulged black eyelid shut his left eye. His mother caressed his battered face and comfortingly asked him, "Where does it hurt more?"

Quietly and scared, he replied, "Nawh, it's okay".

Curious she compressed her eyebrows, she felt his face and said, "Tell me if it hurts you."

He looked away and up to a moisture-filled cloud and said, "Nawh, it's just that I can't see."

Reassured, she replied, "Here's some ice to hold over it."

Still confounded, sloughy, he stared at a certain rain and countered, "It's ahwite, it'll go away."

She hesitated, as if by guilt, and low-hearted said, "I'm going to *Las Olas* to buy some cotton. Just stay cool and safe inside of our house and take an aspirin to lower your swelling."

A spark of energy arose within him when he exclaimed, "Hey wait! Do you have ten dollars?" On public welfare and short on cash, she replied, "What do you need ten dollars for?"

Embarrassed, he whispered, "So I can buy me an ice-cream bar."

Our little homie's words bent her knees and broke her floodgates as she gave him twenty food stamps so that he may split it with his younger sister who remained in tremendous shock and afraid for having witnessed their continuous dramatic lifestyle. She hugged and re-assured her two children that their dad is in the slammer and will not hurt anyone anymore, and they split ways.

She could not go to their convenience store; her feet would not help her as a gloomy dark-gray sky announced an immediate downpour. Their mother, already feverish from a long walk soaked and frozen yesterday, silent and desperate, walked away.

NOXS-TOWN

Born in Honduras, Central America, their parents migrated to *el norte* with a simple vision: for their three children to accomplish a fair education. Limited on money, they hopped on a cross-country bus ride for Guatemala's frontier, *Esquipula*. Their dad and mom with three kids, Moe at ten, Maru at nine and Jacks at eight. Passports, identifications and fares handy, within seventy-two hours they made it to Tijuana's border, hired a *coyote* who immediately stuffed them in a Chevy Nova, crossed San Fuego's Customs' checkpoint and headed to southern Califas to begin their ever-popular "American Dream."

They arrived at Maplewood, Califas, Los Diablos County's west side. A populace of just above 100,000 in a blend of Whites, Blacks, Hispanics, Asians and other races. However, within Maplewood is a reduced and poorer subsection, Noxs-Town, where almost every *marketa* has a Latin name as is ordinary to read on their gastronomical commerce: *Burritos, Tacos, Tortas, and Quesadillas.* It is also normal to see menu choices of *Macho Nachos, Charly's Churros, and Best Cold Cerveza.* For its dominant language is English, Spanish, and Spanglish.

This annexed city is barely minutes east of Los Diablos

International Airport. At around eleven years of age, we used to jump with laughter as we saw this continuous flow of airplanes that arrived and departed. At night, we loved to play Guess That Plane!—American! Continental! United! *Cops!* We dreamed that one day we would own one to travel around the globe as our geographical proximity lent us this unique opportunity, as immigrants from different Latin-American countries, some of us longed to return home. Night flights were special as some passengers' silhouettes appeared in between windows—that is how low those cockpit captains propelled their contaminated vapor trails over us.

Every evening, flows of different jet engines, simultaneously two or three police helicopters that whirled and hovered, and not a crash amongst their closeness or against its voluminous air traffic that entered. It confused and made us curious, as we ran inside to hide under furniture—like scaredy-cats, as our science fiction-like scenery outside unraveled. Firefighters had taught us to do this in case of an earthquake or any major catastrophe, not for helicopters that flied just above us. These choppers illuminated inside and out of our dormitory's windows, bathrooms and roofs at once—and everyone nearby—as they searched for criminals that hid and sprinted into alleys and people's properties. Back then, these bandits used to name those "fireflies'" Public Announcement system "Moses' Word" as it always indiscriminately blasted at everyone—"Stay indoors! Do not come out of your house!"

SIDEWALK UNIVER-CITY

Early in our 1980's decade, elementary education finished, intermediate grades at present, high school loomed and, in accord with our parents' plans and momentum as they held menial employments to sustain us. Around 1985, as teenagers our search began for our unique persona to fit in this new cultural ambience, for example, within our classrooms an aura of unity, discipline, objectives and progress. Outside of our classrooms, lawlessness, drugs, and fights. We contrived to duck under the nearest car or behind fences anytime an explosive device trembled us, opposed to what we had learned in our classrooms how duck under our desks in case of a calamity.

As time passed, we grew apart from our immediate group of friends. Our perennial age of perfectness— when every part of our bodies seems intact—soon erupted pus by way of pimples, chickenpox and herpes. Puberty and physical growth were not our only distinguished changes among our vast clan of young immigrant friends and neighbors but a concealed animosity aroused from an excessive degree of crime outside of our homes—in particular a ricochet of heinous drive-by shootouts and on-demand high-level vandalism acts.

We grew around this city forasmuch of our tender age, and in a sense, our route became somewhat of a choice to select which of our teenage criminal circles we would join. That is, most of our demographical peers dropped out of our musical band courses, our athletic teams, and afterschool paint shops. Truly, mobsters crept up everywhere and targeted, attracted, and enrolled at-risk teenagers just as military recruiters sat at our secondary academies doing likewise. And our teacher's keen perceptive knowledge still guided us, "Yale, he insisted. You must make it to Yail. E Pluribus Unum; can you guys pronounce or remember that?" As class clowns, our team's soccer ball struck our teacher's torso while he wrote on a blackboard, "I will graduate from Yale." *Ka-boom!* There was always a first time to land at our principal's detention room for various periods, thus, legally skipping classes.

Until now, our majority of friends had already *jumped-into* the Noxs-Town 13 side—first as sorority, later to increase our peer's commonality, but afterward to make a name for ourselves and, oddly, this intimidated some of us for not doing likewise. Every weekday, end-of-class battles were commonplace besides a false belief that as we patronized this city it gave us an impressive boost to inherit privileges to represent our locals with an added motive to lead this posse to a number one post in criminality amongst its nearest enemies.

At sixteen years old, on one clear and bright summer midday—when our sun is at its peak, three of us strolled through sidewalks and alleyways, within our neighborhood's constricts, we searched for partners as we knocked on their doors just as evangelists awaken people every sunrise. This outing took care of afternoon time, thus we found and waited for them, played Super Mario Brothers, as they showered and dressed with our posses' plain attire: long white t-shirts, over-sized denims and white leather Cortez. Most times, some of them still slept from our previous nights' party and to get them up for another crazy day seemed to be our jobs as some of our mothers would in a sarcastic tone say, "Ya'll gonna find some work now to get a legal paycheck?"

Our transformation into adulthood within extreme and risky boundaries, we instinctively perceived our dangerous ambience, as witnesses to its drug deals, arm robberies, and acts of violence. Eventually, this city's name became our lifestyle, passion, wretchedness, and our devious character that caused trouble to everyone who crossed our hell-bound roadway. We became synonymous with murder, drug and firearms traffic, and zany wicked attacks on local citizens. Some of us taunted, "Talk-the-talk—walk-the-walk," to signify that excessive boast did not produce any merits whereas our real credit, or *stripes*, is appreciated in our amount and degree of lawlessness, whether for *our hood's* props or to solidify our personal criminal résumé. Our lifelong adage:

> Click—Bang! Click—Bang!
> Big West Side Noxs-Town Gang
> We Kill for Thrills and Party for Chills
> We Never Die—We Multiply!

As with most anti-social undergrounds, we used monikers to conceal our birth names. One of ours, *Peelainsky*, posed a medium size, dark and stocky, and every time he did a stint at any juvenile hall, he would come out with rock-solid biceps, flexible abs and a body-builder's nape. We believed that he *was* a true Mexican descendent though resembled a blend of African, Samoan or Arab ancestry because he spoke with a sputtered Spanglish idiom that made him difficult to understand, and this made us uncertain of which municipality he *really* belonged to; we accepted him anyway. He was serious, dedicated, and silently did his dirty deeds, daily.

This same day, a couple of us went out in search of fun as two more homeboys joined us as our habit was to drink beer, smoke weed, get wild and wacky. As we traveled on foot to every corner of our hood, we ran into *Corky* as he crossed Maplewood Avenue and appeared like an alcoholic's redeemer for he loved to possess a wine bottle and corkscrew—that he used as a shank. He always explored ways to unscrew any type of alcohol beverage and blithely say, "Ain't no shame in my famed pop!—pop!—pop!— opening game." Champagne bottles were his competence and on some nights, he would hide to pop its cork off—slyly insinuated a shotgun blast that sent us tumbling to the asphalt seeking cover.

Our third attached urchin was Pugs. We had tried to name him Midget but could not because we considered that upon his *fisted baptism* to augment our posse's prodigies he stubbornly repeated, "Nopey—Dopey! I ain't gonna be humiliated by our homegirls." However, our molls needed not laugh at his stingy height, rather, at his oversized trousers and jerseys, as he resembled a springy, rattled, desktop bubblehead. Besides, Midget already belonged to another homeboy of about an inch less in stature but from a different clique—and these duplicated fast.

One curiosity about Pugs was his drunken derive into a prankster, as he hugged, touched and ultimately kissity-kissing-kissy, a kiss for this and a kiss for that, so this subtle softy attitude toward us made Peelainsky skittish, abstain, and ignore our camaraderie. We envied Corky's girlfriend therefore, he always reminded Pugs of her faithfulness but emphasizing a web of undue caresses. Anyhow, tough as titanium, our timely unimagined conjecture did not realize, that is, whether our hoodlum was a sanguinary stout short dog or a gay mewing Midget, we never found out though his telltale micro-expressions spoke in sentimental macro-heights.

As in any group of young adults, we were rare at this age, for none of us had yet any legal authorizations to seek employers. Astounded, somehow and in some way, someone always pulled out *the dough* to party this day away as a seasonal zone-line Zephyr with a glorious reddish-yellow panorama dawned on our Pacific Coast horizon refreshing us.

As our evening's splendid sunset vanished, Peelainsky, Corky and Pugs alongside, we started on foot as we leaned backwards in naughty *zoot-suit* style while tagging our initials in our quotidian walkways between one-hundred-fourth and one-hundred-eleventh streets. A couple of blocks into our stroll we ran across three more homeboys at Noxs-Town Park and kicked it with them in its picnic space for a while as we talked glib. One of them was past his fiftieth birthday, a veteran, our waned clique. Crouched next to him, a mid-thirties homeboy rolled a couple of zigzags with weed, and our lookout is around fifteen years of age with straight back black hair.

After about an hour, our initial tight four continued to stroll, the three hoodies stayed behind, as we pushed our way to a nearby well-known kickback and one of our many hideouts, *las tumbas,* the tombs. As usual, one ice-cold forty-ounce led to a dozen more and, afterwards, we became too drunk to stand upright and penniless for additional forties and to persist on our daily togetherness and rambunctious way.

At eleven o'clock that same night, our alcohol's and hash's fallout altered our minds and weaved us sideways as we bumped and tightly held our arms to balance ourselves when unexpectedly we began to evolve a rushed plan for a local beer heist. Our party will not finish before midnight, someone mumbled and implied, *"Let's hit Las Olas."* Someone else immediately foreboded a response, "No way! Not our go-to mini-market."

We convinced and instigated ourselves with anticipative illusions of our already formed game plan for a *quickie* to steal more booze. We arrived to our targeted liquor market and once inside headed straight to its cashiers' counter where a young and shy, caramel-tint roundish female adolescent—whom we only knew by word-of-mouth as Maria. She stood erect behind her counter, serious yet attentive, and upon our arrival, she started to caress her straight long black hair and, without anyone else inside, gave us an appraised stare accompanied by a gracious gleam of her perfect teeth and—to an extent, she relished as she saw customers as she began to audit a bundle of cash. In a short time, everyone began to giggle as our homeboys flirted and this insincere show of fondness flushed her teddy-bear face, and in turn, her trustful smile widened as her gleamed brown eyes circulated the ceiling lights.

With our petty theft underway, Pugs and Corky charmed and sidetracked Maria while Peelainsky and I split between isles and headed straight to a refrigerated area to grab a case of Budweiser each, one of us will sneak out, we figured, without a glitch from her.

Outside of Las Olas Market, heist fulfilled we teemed our egos and headed back to our hideout as we carried two beer cases and joked aloud, "It's *tax* time." This was our way to harass and intimidate an absent Asian owner, or anyone that performed business within our beloved vile city.

At our hangout, an abandoned crank house adjacent to a sidewalk, a front yard, and a murky and crummy garage. We had chosen this dark hidden place because policemen would not walk in there. And more than that, its broken horizontal door creaked as it slid and it shut halfway which allowed us to peep outside at unaware pedestrians. Once seated inside, we chilled to reminisce our hasty life's span—pin-pointedly about our homeboys who were locked-up, had gotten shot or fled a crime scene, skipped town or deported. Within minutes, our three older homeboys arrived with a basket full of liquors and drugs as well, and the oldest of them, visibly asphyxiating, snatched out a *fix kit* that had been stashed somewhere throughout our darkness.

In any event, our youngest quickly removed one of his shoestrings and tied it around an upper arm of our sweat-filled fidgety aging man. As this transpired, their middle-age man brought forth a cigarette lighter out of his pocket, ignited it, and everyone saw this intravenous junky surgery.

Again, their youngest pulled a silver teaspoon out of their kit, emptied a grain of tar that they referred to as the big H, mixed half a teaspoon of whiskey onto it and with their lighter flambé it and dissolved it into its pure opium form. Their fix was ready to insert a vein.

Now, their youngest, keenly apprehensive of our veteran's weak and wart nodular freeway of veins at his forearm, asked to come closer. Afterwards, this youngster used its syringe's barrel to vacuum a coal-like globule and pinched our veteran's worn vein and, as in a time capsule, injected their oozy Eych into his slippery vein as every drop flushed its cocktail of blood and junk; the big H. Heroin, high, and hallucination heaped our older homeboys henceforth. How-not-to idiocy we had not yet learned in any school.

Chitchat over; their two oldest men, snoozed on-and-off while indoctrinated us with regards of *nuestro varrio,* our ghetto. They regurgitated our genesis and of our turf's bloody grapples and how to progress nowadays. At times, contemporary families that had transformed—and persisted—to carry this vicinity into a stately recognized mob: our malicious Maxias', drug lords Lapiz's, and violent Valentinos.

Notwithstanding, our crux of experiences quickly turned into a query of my family's history, my integrity, and faithfulness for our shared responsibility to acquire admission, self-respect, and infamous prestige with, and, from them. They insisted to remain true and obedient to our *hard cores*—as these are our men who had gone full circle, some of them even paid its ultimate price of lifetime imprisonment, and death. Our allegiance to our homies' herald, our ol'-skool of hard 'nnox they instructed.

Anyway, our oldest, who possessed tweety-like but diluted eyeballs, as their heroin high weakened him, or from his natural characteristic, was bald and had a Marlboro mustache. His dress was a black football jersey, slacks twice his size and sneakers. In the same obedient way I sat in detention classrooms, gazed at their hateful mimics and nodded—as a hairnet held my hair tightly backwards—silently engaged to their indicative accidence brainwash yet afraid of our Original Gangsters' tragic accounts.

Upon criminals' code-of-conduct night class, in total drunkenness and high-as-kites, our three Ohw-Gees lent Peelainsky, Corky and Pugs a wrecked hot-wired primed hatchback *Gremlin* to return to our same mini-market and make one last beer-run before it closed at two past midnight. We drove to it and together tumbled inside; however, a paunchy Asian man stood by a cash register and angrily gestured to a sheriff to look at the store's corner cameras as his police partner closed-in on Maria to interrogate her. We panicked and aborted atrocity. Corky sprinted through a dark alley as we jumped back into our borrowed car but its engine did not buzz because its ignition raw wires were in a spaghetti knot over its dashboard thus permitted a fraction of a second for the cops to look around and catch up on our shoplifting.

Busted!

CAMP SNOOPY

Three days after our arrests, nine just convicted punks for different crimes are off onto three to nine-month sentences in various Los Diablos County Youth Halls; Peelainsky and Pugs headed elsewhere on different black-and-white minivans. Our transport van—with its grand Los Diablos Sherriff's Department logos on its sides, is perhaps to highlight us to society's sane citizens as its new wave of sleaze-balls. We exited Maplewood Minors' Townhouse at around 10:00 A.M. and now we are on Interstate 405 attempting to go north, but paralyzed.

Common everyday rush-hour traffic, bumper-to-bumper boringness, window-to-window lookie-loos, and ridiculous radio-to-radio frenzy. Various boom boxes played the Dow Jones, K-Globe 101, Lottery Channel, Mexican rancheras and modern hip-hop as everyone wishes to listen louder than their next driver does. A few of them finding refined music to transform their neck-and-neck stress and anxiety into a joyful and relaxed trip.

Behind us, a white KIA sedan with two old nuns in its front seats and two sexy young ones in its backseats hyperactively reverberated and manually articulated Hail Maries at us to simulate their holiness with rosaries and well-intended pietism. They appeared to ask, tell, or solicit Saint Sebastian to maintain us far from their vehicle and to lead us in our right lane. They seemed nervous that we might incur an unnecessary accident with them as they swerved and switched lanes yet, like us, headed nowhere. At this sight, one of our fellows interjects, "Catch 'yall in our camp's church cherubs!"

We, on a hell bound way, weave up a river, as they say. Three Hispanics, two African-Americans, and two White-Americans. Two young molls accompany us, a Latina and a Black, handcuffed and not speaking one word to anyone but only stare ahead.

Our van remained cold throughout our trip and inconvenient for sightseeing through its windows as iron crossbars and mesh wires hindered our views. Although we have individual cuffs at our wrists to restrict our shifting postures, we broke our silence with personal and polite social gossip as when we date a newfound friend. As first-timers, our main query emerged amongst us, how will it be like *in there?* Some of our replies, "Man! I'm gonna bomb on a first nigga comes-up to mah face." A flimsy youngster said, "First thing I'm doin'-is finding a way to run out of there—I ain't staying in here no nine months." A third fellow added, "I'm gonna lift weights, eat and get big to get back with my baby mamma. I'm not chasing dad to *the pen*."

One blonde boy was a timid, skinny, puny boy with rimless bifocals as he read a *Laptop Geek Magazine.* Mostly everyone slid back to meditate, lost in thought, an attempt to configure our dreadful decency. Our techie immersed in his mag, scanned it, paged it, and held it tight as if it would fly off our encased van. No one looked his way. Our reality conversed away from our home's comforts to a spine-chilling mood of encampments' fistfights, and this slowly silenced us.

Under supposed regular vehicular speeds, this is a one-hour drive to Mid-city's La Verne Mountains but with our fluctuating traffic jam, to arrive before dinnertime would possibly be an entreat to welcome us. Theretofore, some of us slept, pondered, and clowned about our non-gallant farts. Outside, high above our van and hardly visible is a Good-Year blimp hummed and brightly flashed a "Go Badgers!" message over our congested vehicular serpentine. It will perform a round-trip flight and we will remain stranded here along a fixed post-prison date with our dear nuns.

Ultimately, we arrived at campground around four p.m., after we dropped off our two girls in the "females only" side of this camp. We were tired and subdued from our prolonged trip as some of us kept asking if we may get off to stretch our legs yet without wasting a nanosecond, our driver's companion—noticing our hyper-activeness, urged, "Don't—no one step out of this van!" We were only anxious to get our program *rollin'* along. As soon as our driver parked our van, his companion walked carelessly into camp's headquarters with our court records tightly tucked under his left arm to check-in with its administrators.

Twenty more minutes of idle delay, still handcuffed, had gone when our driver returned to lead us to our superintendents' quarter. Metal cuffs removed, we split in twos to meet our counselors—who had been preselected, and were ready to assist us, legal folders cuddled on their forearms. After our brief rudimentary interviews, they brought us together again in a Cinema Room and played a Video Home System movie, *"Scared Straight"*. Its preface is about a dramatic real-life penitentiary documentary intended to dissuade and deviate early youth criminality. After we watched it, for sure, every one of us sat quiet, petrified, mummified.

Near six p.m., on this facility's uphill side windows, we saw how a last bit of sunlight shimmered between tower-like greenwoods as it announced its orangey-red afternoon's end. Still, even camp personnel protected themselves with thick winter coats while they ran errands in and out of various offices. We were hungry as our meals awaited warm and ready, but they had said that we must first stop at our new barbershop followed by our hot showers. We cannot walk inside of this camp in civilian clothes; only county personnel and state accredited persons may do so.

Ultimately, they made us ready to proceed as we dressed in blue jeans, pale navy blue button-down shirts, heavy shinbone-high waterproof boots and fiber-made safety helmets. Besides our assignment's gear, we were shoved an army belt, a flask, and blankets. As this transpires, one kid of about twelve years of age sobbed when his amount of stress and consternation peaked and rudely rejected his chattels. In delirious ante, he shrilled, "Where's my mama! I want to go home!" His counselor hastily approached this kid's squabble, appeased him and we started fast-forward into our private property again.

We met our kitchen staff while we ate a plentiful dinner, which calmed us, then returned to watch an introductory video that outlined this camp's manual: rules, reliability, consequences, laundry and sick-call procedures, proper gymnasium accessory control and conform to a caste comport.

Their strictest emphasis is our out-of-bound areas—an invisible radius to roam our compound by virtue that if found beyond *it* we will receive an added administrative sentence of attempted escape and lose this camp's great privilege, which is, fenceless. Any object not provided by our camp's personnel is consider contraband with an attached write-up and punitive action to compensate its make and length of such a piece. We are never to unite with known gang accomplices or walk in packs of three of our own race. Bravo; bedtime.

"Rise—N—Shine!" Hollered Mister Balloon through an assemblage of overhead loudspeakers that echoed at exactly 5:45 A.M. "Sit up straight on the edge of your bed. Don't move—don't look at your homies—don't ask me anything—just sit and look my way." Unfettered, he seizes our inactivity to daylight, "You have fifteen minutes to fix your bed, get dressed, wash-up and get back to your bunk and sit-up again in the same side you always do. Nothing has changed since yesterday."

One-hundred-plus consolidated dwarfed rats curled under our covers and struggle to open our eyes—as some of us did not budge at our airport-volume loudspeakers—to at least, remove our warm blankets. Easily, one-hundred-and-forty-four filled beds yet on any given night, someone would ache and wake up in a nearby hospital. In contrast, on our early rise, a sad sight of bare mattresses upon which our buddies once slept and their empty lockers awaited a new arrival. Some of us were still deep in dreamland; our staff refers this sleep state our lazy zonked zone. It is our neighbors' unofficial responsibility to alert our next youth in a choreographed domino-effect sequence but we never arose as intended.

Altogether, twelve Native-Indian labels—such as Arapahos and Comanches—jutting from our roofs to indicate every assembly of twelve beds alongside our extensive wooden cabin-like dormitory, and, at center, an imaginary line that split our tribes on opposite reflective halves. Still in our middle divider, a Control Center, two counselors overlooking our whereabouts and re-directing anyone who thwarted directives or ones pretending not to hear.

This wide open-air camp's design is for first-time non-violent offenders; it looks like a mountainous picnic park, a sober cozy livelihood and much unlike juvenile hallways where chastises are single-man cells. In certain ways, we became convivial. Racial, ethnic and religious integration was a rule to practice but not to include street gangs.

"You all know my routine," gruffly announced Mister Balloon, "It's 6:00 A.M., formulate a straight line at that door with an *Exit* sign over it." We are supposed to form it at our barrack's central double-door to wait for an escort to our cafeteria to eat and we flunked, as a few of us did not adhere to it. A few youngsters' horseplay distracted us.

At 6:30 A.M., we returned from breakfast and onto our beds to sit straight and to be re-briefed. Mister Balloon will be today's coordinator, as we know that he is firm, and watchful as he guides our every step. Our fellows that have been in here longer said that he *always* wears his army military jacket, "You have until seven to use the toilettes, showers, dress in work uniforms, return to your bunk and remain seated quietly until further notice—so go!"

A bright sunrise underway at 7:00 A.M., our camp's president, a mature and astute resident, approached every tribe with a clipboard's lengthy list of names of those who will labor outside of our grounds and facetiously yapped them as he began with our Apaches, "Lopez! Troop Adam 3! Butler! Troop Bro-foe! Chavez! Van Charley's angels! Johnson! Van Denver dikes! Henderson! *Pay Crew!*—you lucky $#@&R!"

At 7:15 A.M., we were up, ready in our designated platoons, and *marched* outwards to troopers who waited alongside their carpool vans with identifying placards attached to their windshield's wipers. Six drivers headed to different sites of various land sizes to perform traditional and bizarre jobs though their most mischief was how they unequally distributed labor and wages. In fact, not everyone was on a payroll for different reasons, for example, social or judicial restitution or retribution. Furthermore, several of us did not receive any money for our toils, as "camp labor" *was* some of our magistrate's final word.

At around 7:30 A.M., we were supposed to ride out of here although before we did so, they aligned us for an after-meal calories burn-up: two laps around our baseball track, fifty pushups, and a threefold of twenty jumping jacks— cherry pickers—and squats. Once on our parking lot, we had to stand firm, soldier posture, next to our respective vans, and wait yet conformed of today's drudgery along its pack of heavy agrarian tools and our drivers that would haul us.

At exactly 8:00 A.M., subsequently we rolled out of our driveway and headed to our terminals for unpaid duty. Most likely, it would be a local recreational area although it may be any public property anywhere within Los Diablos County though almost certainly the Franklyn Bosselli Regional River or Don Dimas' Dog Park to lift feces into a poop bag, classify it, register it to secure extra amenities and a graduate's paycheck.

———

Thankfully, our busy overworked week passed successfully and no controversies or write-ups, as disciplinary rules are stricter when we are outside of camp because we boldly represent our various governments. Graciously, fatigued, exuberated and proud, we enjoyed it.

Super Saturday's school sessions. Today's extraordinary prominence is that we had more sleep time than on weekdays; we awoke at 8:00 A.M. undisturbed by needless puffed-up demands and ear bursting drills. Still, some of our fellows did not open their eyes to our bright sunshine. Classes begin at 10:00 A.M. and everyone is mandatorily to attend our lecture rooms whether it be for math, science, philosophy or language arts. We have technical shops at our convenience: car mechanics and body repair, industrial welding and painting, residential plumbing and electricity. However, our instructors warn that these vocations are for self-sufficiency and not for us to go breaking into people's properties.

Our General Education Diploma course *is* our most popular as none of us is graduating from any progressive academy, so far. A few of us came in here from our local grade school playgrounds and though not convicted of a certain crime, somehow became involved in one. Aiding and abetting, they said.

Tutor courses are State mandated and regulated; hence, only a life-threatening brain stroke may prevent us from attending. Worse, we do not have many illnesses around here—besides our inherited cold and flu, as everyone is young and tough as Elmwood. Truly, plentiful tasty non-fat food, moderate daily exercise, an honest labor habit and leisure time cannot depress anyone. Our infirmary room is oftentimes empty.

When on our best behavior we fascinate our jumpy camp superintendent. He says that we are not bad kids, only innocent bystanders, he advises, "Learn from your mistakes and you will smoothly graduate out of here." *The sup* is an aged, crouched, wrinkled and lanky yet cheery Irish man with an Einsteinian sloppy drooping curly gold hair. On Sundays, he sprints into our cafeteria dressed in a leprechaun's outfit and oogie-boogies to Mozart waltzes, shamanic trances and the Pee-Wee Herman rap song as he tosses green-color shamrocks candy at us. No one eats those three-leaf clovers because they taught us in a hygiene seminar that candy is bad for our health; they said that it would turn our teeth, fingernails and eyeballs, green. We dared not laugh at his terrified and injury-prone moves because we are aware that no one would tango out of here without his presidential signature on our congratulatory diplomas—so we eat his jawbreakers!

His general bureau' associate is a short, fat, and runny Philippine gofer, Mister Mendez. He habitually wears a black suit and tie and dark sunglasses as if he is a prestigious worldwide trust's president —Welfare—Feed Our Kids or Starved Visionaries. We always receive promises from him that go up in smoke; some of us label it, "Smoker's Art."

Mister Mendez is a time sensitive man. First, he said we will enjoy, in a successive timeframe, a brand-new state-of-their-art theater system in our Cinema Room, never received it. Secondly, he says that if we have a deep desire to resemble John Jay Rambo, without wasting time in our weights' pile, we *need* to use new and digitalized track-and-field apparatus, nowhere in sight. His ultimate promise is to cut our time in half; we wait, lift weights, and wait. What, which, or whose time? Does he refer to our time it takes to drive to-and-from Los Diablos' courthouses mounted on the 405 expressway? "Time", he whispers into our ears, "is expendable." No one knows what *expendable* means—so no one questions it! We only cross our fingers until our time to go home arrives, expendable or not.

Whenever we perceive his overblown false blabs, we always grant him benefits to his distaste and do our best to make his duties more interesting by grinding his gears. That is, we start food fights in our dining cabin; make a daredevil dash down this forest from our weight pit; smuggle in Playboy magazines and masturbate—overwhelmingly at night when our female counselors supervise us. Some of us in our naïve discovery to mature calculate our penises' sizes and create contests to congratulate our fastest ejaculator thusly winner of his bragging spoils the next day. Fortunately, we are within our tender youth compulsiveness, and developmentally sound.

Our mothers tell us we are adorable kids and have not reached adulthood. Our fathers teach us to kick any ones ass if disrespected by anybody. We expect that our growth pains will make Mister Mendez adequately value us. He is unbelievably startled on parents' visiting days as he sees most kids act, well, like kids canting in family. In subsequent manner, on weekends, we request our music of choice in the lounge area, and mostly everyone bumps a camp-shaker of Cypress Hill's "Comprendes, Mendes?" only to inculcate our song across his haughty neurons.

The bus driver that takes us to their masked forced-labor every weekday is in his early forties; a green-eye bristled top-shape Caucasian, light-brown beard and mustache always neatly trimmed. Besides our transport, he is also responsible for maintaining our boundaries at every site—and does not become involved in whatever happens inside of our camp as he anticipates our creepy immoral stories when he softly says, "No-no-no! I don't want to hear what happens in there. My job is to take you out and bring you back—that's all fellas."

Our tiresome doubt is who in this campground gave him guidelines to make us behave as dinky clowns every time we run after our food sacks before lunchtime. Yes, he stops our van at any safe park—as he will not drive into crime-infested territory, and chooses its farthest picnic bench from our vanpool and briskly unleashes us like when puppies sniff fresh air when exiting a kennel, and fatherly says, "One quick lap around *t-h-i-s* park—*a-n-d* back."

They are some of our staff members we interact with daily. Our general medicine doctor—whom we have not seen since our initial physical exams. Every so often, we pretend to feel sick or fake an injury only to encounter his sensual nurse's prescreen sweetness. Though speedy scoundrels that we are, most often we go in their private quarter just to relax, kick-back, feel her tender hands' soft touch then caressing our supposed aching bodies as we listen to her endearments, and as delighted men brag about it at night in our barracks as we fantasize and...compete.

MISTER DWIGHT

"That's em—ahr—dee!" our thirty-year-old homeroom teacher punctuates as he strikes his chalkboard with his wand to recapture our haywire dementia. Not a pitch-black or dark-brown man, only a lesser shade of caramel color, let us just say that our *Perfect Professor* varnished him a luster medium Oak. Slim as a sapling, athletic, humorous, and a cheery charismatic personality. He speaks with a semi-stutter of rapper's delight verbiage and academic rhetoric. Outside of our lecture room, we misname him—just as we have nicknames for every staff member, "Teacher Tamarind." We agree that he is better off with impersonations of, or as a performer of stand-up doubles for known actor and comedian Teddie Murffy.

Mister Dwight is sassy, dandy, and always sports neat golf attire and fancy lecture bifocals. Every time he sits at *his* desk, lowers his loops to his thin nose tip, and says, "Ya'll don't play golf *doo*—yall?" As he surveys everyone, he answers, "Hee—hee—hee, *i-y-h* didn't think so. Ya'lls got a weight pile to become like *ugh-ugh—Arnold* but just don't-go-roun'-sayin' what-he-say, *'I-I'll be back!'* Cause *t-h-e-y—they* will b-r-ing you back. Hee—hee. My dear students, I'm no Tiger Woods but I's got *games* also—hee—hee—hee."

With twelve students to tutor, he is apt to recognize our newbie every time when he takes roll call. "Okay, h-o-l-d on class. There is a new name he-egh-oun-ma-list—hee—hee—hee. I bet any one of yaa-lls I can point'em out with-ma-iyhs closed—hee—hee!"

Our teacher soothes us when he speaks smoothly and never raises his voice at anyone. Once, he announced, "Si-silence please. I-I must be straightforward with you young men, citizens of this, *ahumm!* camp; this memo comes from Sacramento's Executive Orchestrator of Education—yes! The *o-n-e* up there in very high places signing my paychecks, his message is that you all—*he-he—a-humm*, pertain to a privileged sector of coachable plebs, nuw-namely—Learners with Special Tutor Assistance." Then he says, "Do-do-do—any of yall have any qu-questions? A classmate hyperactively raised his hand and yelled, "I do!—Mister Dee! Can we still climb and win our camp's Honor Roll List to go our houses sooner?" Like children inside of a circus, everyone burst into infantile laughter.

Mister Dwight again strikes his blackboard's middle—though he always targets his prescribed "Mr. D", and docile yet jovially, apologizes for he is not Yahveh to judge us—and immediately re-hooks our naive curiosity when he subtly speaks his mind, as we seem to telepathize:

Mr. D: Hee—hee—hee. Slow learners! Slow learners!

Our Homie: Catch me once shame on you. Catch me twice shame on me.

"Hee—hee—hee. Slow learners!"

"Three arrests in three months for the same crime."

"Hee—hee—hee. Slow learners!"

"No one taught me History."

"Hee—hee—hee. Slow learners!"

"God is long-suffering."

"Hee—hee—hee. Slow learners!"

"Our car was keyless and borrowed from unknown friends."

"Hee—hee—hee. Slow learners!"

"My friends are cool."

"Hee—hee—hee. Slow learners!"

"It is not what you think Mister Tamarind Man."

"Slow learners—hee—hee—hee. Ya'lls ready to go back *h-o-m-e* now? Alright, let us just wait nineteen seconds more—hee—hee—hee! Else I get in trouble for lettin' ya'lls go early—he—he—he! I'm keeping *bo-b-o-t-h* of my eyes on my waterproof Timex; can you guys see what time it is. I'm gettin' paid, yous ain't—hee—hee—hee!"

Hee-hee, secretly we adore to use epithets as we mimic, criticize, and ridicule our assortment of exemplary faculty.

"Klahw—Class dismissed."

A JUDICIAL CAVE

"Then the prisoners would in every
way believe that the truth
is nothing other than the shadows of those
artifacts."—*Plato (c. 428-348 B.C.)*[*]

Who am I to judge? A simple selective process to merge a twelve-panel jury from a numerous pool of law-abiding citizens whom one picks in the same manner that we meet persons on webpages such as Facebook: Like; Unlike; Block. Our peer selective process is tricky as both representatives attempt to assemble their twelve best persons to convince and vote favorably in their upcoming pros-and-cons debates and truth-or-deceit search to conduct their case at hand towards a victory, respectively.

These city dwellers arrived from diversified sectors of greater Los Diablos County and now most of this dozen persons are perched upright inside of a jury box sternly as they scrutinize their defendant; their youngest appear laidback—and they are my best prospects for a hung jury. Two alternates: a retired person, perhaps, and a college student, maybe, posted likewise outside of their exclusive area, notetaking utensils handy.

Everyone waits for a judge to appear, our jurors just sit in that box like colorful pigeons, eternally, it seems. Our older jurors remain motionless and exhibit expressions as when one conceals a child's favorite toy. In contrast, our young abstract jurors, as if their thought of their boyfriends or girlfriends is more enthusiastic than their sneaky duty in here. A fact is definite, an undented and showy impatience to have their twiddling itchy fingers on a latest i-phone instead of those notebooks. And their immediate post of their newest dry blog or tweet, "We Hung-'um!"

This theatrical orchestra appear vexed, bitter, and unwilled to predominate its focal sphere—up to now they are, and my fate is in their control. They already know my charges of graffiti, vandalism, and possession of gang bandanas, purely misdemeanors though they carry possible jail time, for sure.

A convoluted legal, bureaucratic, and sort-of war analysis and decision-riddled stunt as prosecutor and public defender out-strategize themselves; our first instigates for captivity while our opponent begs for leniency. In contrast, for those of us unfamiliar with Law and Order it appears as though our State has a slight leverage to win this turgid war, as their duty is to protect our public's safety; unlike our defense attorneys whose flawed social percepts seems as if they protect, by all means, an individual accused of an illegal offense, a criminal. Moreover, Uncle Sam *is* our overhead, and as such, retains a massive legal lever over our average citizens, besides; they are to secure our peace in our communities. *E pluribus Unum* is their bond.

This panels' service began when their names was infused in a master list of about fifty honest gents of different backgrounds, ethnicities, grade levels, ages and lifestyles. Their time for evidence exactness and ethical judgment is now: guilty, innocent, or *unsure*.

A fortyish female court clerk commenced our process as she attentively announced guidelines to our twelve finalists: "To all jurors, please state your full name and area of residence, profession or current employment and marital status. Have you or anyone in your family ever been a victim of a crime? Have you or has anyone in your family ever been charged and/or convicted of a crime? Is there any personal or medical reason why you feel that you cannot serve as a juror in this case? If so, please explain."

When no juror pronounced any pretext for relief of social duty, our trial made headway.

From an opposite spectrum and of near importance, behind this trial occurs a negative record of such court presence for social misconduct. For instance, recently out of juvenile camp and having just reached adulthood, am again seated on an accused corner's accumulating litigious suits. As in many times before, diverted and dissociated with age-old disturbed thoughts and prejudices about our complex judicial administrative views, a need for inner justice, yet keenly focused as our good-will-to-do citizens answered our tribunal's questionnaire.

On occasions, one of them blunders a humorous response and, in accord, caused a surround-like gossipy laughter that pervaded to our audience, everyone except me. In effect, every time my lips flinched a smile, our jurors immediately stopped their laughter, turned solemn, and rubbernecked me again. At a standstill, we just sat there, idly, with deductive inspectors' surgical gazes from inside of their privy zone. In cynical view, from our public defenders' corner, our dirty dozen came forth as a spectacular, thriving and screaming, philosophical anthropological live pose of Leonardo Da Vinci's composite, jackhammers in hands.

In contrast, one of our jurors utters an honest answer or a thoughtful silliness, and so with a suppressed inward quiet laugh—a half-smirk—they quickly returned their reproached gazes. They remained speechless though inadvertently implied, what in hell is pinned inside of this man's mind or what is wrong with it?—for that matter. Our demeanors speak louder than terse responses, as if they whispered, "This is a court trial for goodness's sake—and we got you!" Every aspect appeared as a boggled dilemma where my only choice was to sit upright, stay calm, silent and serious—a real outcasts' display. Meanwhile, underneath my toes vibrated and my soul itched to join on their jokes too.

Everyone in our courtroom patiently awaits, as we listen and survey how our task unfolds, and our male judge shared his friendliness as a professional partaker in his arena. He spoke to our lead juror, "This morning, *a-h-h*, driving into our parking lot, the attendant asked if I had a valid pass and I said 'of course I have a valid pass—I'm the judge!'"—and everyone except their suspect erupted in laughter.

At whimsy intervals, our jury resemble nice, generous, laborious and honest-to-heart humans, but when they deliberate, they mutate into our common Homo sapiens, convoluted and unpredictable. True, they did not break our laws; I did. Hallelujah that my life's turbulent prior arrests is unknown to them for adult reasons that we may make presumptive stereotypes whenever seeing a person for a first time. As for now, unheard to their ears is a history of psychological prefabricates, for example, an abandoned infant, an absent-minded and oft-troubled child, a variety of incessant frontal cortex therapy sessions, and a high school dropout as a teenage run-away. A societal chaff with a grade level F, a definitive for flustered, flimsy, and finished.

Alternately, and most likely, my defender will not even take a minute of our time to remark grandma's hummed biblical lullabies nor her inculcations to tithe at Sabbath Sect and, perhaps most influential, to forgive freely, for its irrelevancy to this trial or *beyond the point*. What, which, or whose point?

After numerous prior misdemeanor and felony verdicts that resulted with stints in various local juvenile cribs and county jails that anticipated a two-year state prison term—tough evenly successful in those exams with above-average grades. These previous drastic encounters with police agents—sometimes at gunpoint—happened under twenty-one years of age. An all-encompassed social misfit and our precise contender of nine-out-of-ten administrative prerequisites for another penitentiary tour. A return to sender with a needless cash on delivery sticker yet satisfied Califas' Rehab Rangers lifetime subscriber number: YA-65544.

AQUARIUM DICTUM

"Freedom is the right to tell people what they
don't want to hear."—*George Orwell (1903-1950)*

Tuesday's Eve Football Must-See Game, score: Darlas'
Ranchers 37 and Blue Bay Backers 35. However, tomorrow
at sunrise, a prosecutor at our local courthouse will await
for me to negotiate a plea bargain, and surrender. A month
ago, an infraction for conducting under alcohol's influence
has me in this dilemma. In spite of that, the televised show
is in its overtime quarter filled with enthusiasm and can't-
miss plays though blurred because that previous incident
nags at me.

While the special event plays, along a couple of beers,
quickly snapped out of it because now is an appropriate
juncture to stop and think things through. That is, to drink
alcohol before the start of a viable jail sentence is not a bright
idea. For one, sickness from its hangover will not help my
attentiveness—and two, risking not showing up. Regardless,
this occasion is a relief to some of that stress and will do me
just fine for this games' sake then a peaceful night's sleep.

December 23, 2003; 7:30 A.M. it is cold and gloomy,
its wintriness befits December's last days. Standing on

Crenshaw and Rosecrans boulevards corner, our public bus has not arrived as it always runs on schedule and frequently—my desperation is mounting, but who is in a hurry to get locked-up? Our civic center is less than an hour away.

8:30 A.M. A Maplewood's Municipal Courthouse Commissioner will administer my misdemeanor infraction. A prosecutor pre-arranged a deal to pay a fine, court costs and retribution, to enroll in a state mandated alcohol dependence program and to serve two days in the men's county jail. His package round off is seven years of parametric autonomy, unsupervised disciplinary terms and to spare my driver's license.

Last night's six-pack and late-ending high-flying football coverage left me with an awkward drowsiness and restlessness; though my plan is to sleep through their intake process, if possible, at our new Twin Titans Corrective Facilities. As an ex-con, my awareness is that if every trivial cue goes well, within forty-eight hours should reach a dormitory, a gym mattress, and out to our streets again.

Inside of the bus amongst three more passengers and on my way to court, an irked puzzled thought to exit and return home or to run off anywhere else, except into our county jail. A contrary thought is that our law master will dictate an arrest warrant and police agents will begin to look for and re-arrest me; also not a bright idea. A pros and cons measure of every component, truly, a decisive course to choose before my stand in front of the man's throne. Lost in thought, a predominant equation is that this easy transaction will extend in a negative sequence for a failure to appear; conversely, to comply with our courts' mandates will aid to keep a clean slate and to restrain myself from future run-ins with our men in blue for fear of its consequences.

In a sane state of mind, convinced for a righteous maneuver, walked into our courtroom dressed in a pair of old beige Dockers, a tee shirt, and sneakers. Anyone who has served time in this county jail knows that upon release no one has a collateral to receive his or her same clothes returned. That is, our wardrobe *trustees* are always on the lookout for our best suits to steal, exchange, gamble and sell to pricey inmates, or for *their* own release.

In addition, dressed in typical descriptive aberrant apparel is deceivingly helpful in case of any unforeseen troubles and disputes and disrespectful inmates. Hoodlums will always stick together. Besides, loners are conspicuous and disfavored by gangsters; some introverts remain in danger of vulnerabilities and are targets for seductive hostilities and various abuses by nefarious thugs' ill standards.

Everyone roamed in and out of our courtroom because inside one needs a sweater to keep warm, as its air-conditioner runs at full blast, likewise my escapist thoughts. We have a packed auditorium as our local community files in with long pretentious faces and those already seated stare blankly ahead, perhaps at our attractive historical hanging symbol of *Our Great Seal of Califas* above the man's bench in its courtroom's center.

A hurried well-built male black bailiff, a middle age blonde woman court reporter and an old white woman serves as clerk; everyone plays with sticky notes within their respective stations. Beside them, a few young and well-tailored legal representatives skim a stacked up legal load of reports and files to prioritize their readiness for our arbitrator to enter. From our audiences' view, ninety-nine percent of our court's personnel are of white descent, except our bailiff, who moves up and around their bench as he scouts out papers and randomly glances back in search of a name from their folders to match a person.

Our hall's silence and its unknown eeriness, mysterious men and women seated, we daydream, and wait. Unhesitatingly, an abrupt steady rustle of popcorn as someone makes an unignorably muncher's noise that disturbed our peace; it echoed every inch of our courtroom thus immediately attracted our bailiff's awareness. When he turned toward us and surveyed everyone as if to inculpate a pickpocket, he admonished, "There's absolutely no eating in our courtroom! Put it away or I will lock you in the hold tank until your case comes up." From within us, a black woman in her mid-forties howled back, "Aye-wuhnt-eat'n-ahnnethang!" He quickly turned to her and said, "I *wasn't* talking to you *ma'am*." She shrugged, put her bag of chips inside of her purse and closed it.

10:00 A.M., no one has come out of chambers, we have been in here two hours and daring to flee, well, my mind has already driven past a desert's roadside flashy billboard, "Welcome to Fabulous Las Vegas". Insane, veritable and indivisible, that a simple careless ticket has everyone under indirect arrest. If time is money and fuel, surely, we already lost some of it parked in here, aloof.

Withal eventualities, a draped-in-black intercessor appears from a side door and walks up to his bench. A bald, light skin, seven-foot man with glasses sits on his office chair then with a soft, secure yet polite tone of an Airbus captain greets everyone that convened and announces today's first file:

"Deborah Montgomery, are you in here?"

A black woman in her mid-twenties stood up, faced his bench and answered, "Yes-Siree!"

"Failure to make a complete stop at an intersection ma'am."

Abruptly, she said, "I did stop your honor! Only thang I did wuz cross those white lanes in front of my car. Then police officers gonna pull me over five blocks down the road to-give-me-a-ticket!"

"Miss Montgomery, when you arrived at the stop sign did you do your three humpty dumpties?

Doubtful and hesitant, she answered, "Nawh. I ain't got no dumpties your honor."

He smiled and said, "One humpty-dumpty, two humpty-dumpties, three humpty-dumpties."

Skeptical, she replied, "Nawh. I ain't never heard you have to do bumptie-dumpties on no road."

Inquiringly, our caped peacemaker added, "Do you think the police officer was wrong when he handed you this traffic citation?"

Thoughtful, she answered, "Nawh. All I'm sayin' is that I *did* stop and I *don't* deserve no ticket."

Assured, our mediator sets logic and consequence to everyone's forefront, "Miss Montgomery, you must bring your vehicle to a halt to prevent accidents—and—you've just admitted that you did not do your humpty dumtpies and that you've never heard of them. Do you prefer to pay one-hundred-and-fifty dollars now or do you need an extension?"

She took a deep breath and recognized her self-admitted guilt, confirmed our cloaked umpire's hilarious trap and agreed to pay her fine in two installs as she said, "I ain't got no money to be payin' no silly *tickets* to no one."

He continued to adjudicate friendliness as he advised her, "Very well, have a nice day and don't forget your humpty dumpties at every stop sign. Now go to the second floor and make your payoff plans."

"Alright, next case on calendar. Please step forward sir. Client is present and according to this docket, he is here to surrender on a joint accord. Alright, that's five days in the men's county jail."

In a haste rose my arm, "It's two days your honor."

He took a second view to verify it, then tweaked, "Strike the record, client is correct. He is now sentenced to spend two days in the Twin Titans Corrective Facilities."

Our judge erected himself, sighed, and from his bench he looked at me and announced, "Client has shown good faith, and sir, Christmas is just around the corner so would you like to delay this matter until after holiday season—how about January fifteenth?"

I smiled and said, "No your honor, let's just get this over with but thanks for your offer."

Magistrate's casual farewell, he ended "Alright, merry Christmas and good luck young man."

With a deep inhale, I replied, "Thank you your honor."

Our bailiff approached, pulled out his shiny metal wristlets and…

…Click! Click! Gone!

BRICKS INTERNATIONAL

Everyone who received jail sentences is now in Marshal's Custody and headed downtown on their next vacant carrier, notoriously known as "heels on wheels". An unmistaken black-and-white statuesque Greyhound with poster-size bright gold five-point stars on the sides of its bulldoze structure, we drifted throughout our city locked inside of this bus that is as tantamount as the Titanic on tires, we hitched and dropped off neighborly suspects from local courthouses, jails, and police sub-quarters. A busload formed and every person inside was shackled to their bones without sight of any outside vehicular traffic; only emergency sirens, engines revving and roaring, and cars' honking different tunes that perforated our earlobes. Our metropolitan's tumultuous congestive whirred noise.

Our majority of men eased this crisis as they sang biblical praises or capriciously investigated their court transcripts. Some couples get involved in abstract discussions, and a few bowed and held their scalps in defeated, helpless, dumbfounded postures. We were eager to reach this county jail to stand, stretch, move about and see new faces—and maybe even detect a friend or two for comradery, and to disengage from prisons' truisms. A few young first-timers remained naïve and unwilling to imagine or picture what lies ahead, and in disbelief mocked our recidivists' heads-up stories.

In reality, some of us are short-timers and under a week will get out while thousands must stay in here for a long stint as they defend their felony accusations. About half of our sentenced men have to wait to go up state and three of them are lifers who will never enjoy unobstructed sunlight and natural air again.

Our bus transfer from local courthouses to the county jail felt like a cordial ride to distress—as when we carpool around our neighborhoods picking up strangers—and to salute our *real* neighbors. Thus, we interweaved various Los Diablos' inner cities—we apperceive our whereabouts by query of every new arrestee on-board.

Withal our uncertainty, my mind reverberates: "Intake procedure, dormitory check-in, three meals a day." *Shoots.* Another brush with authorities, however, this time there was no need for a police task force to arrest, drag, and club me into a backseat of a patrol car. This anew arrest is a dire lesson to digest a beneficial experience as it is now or never to make necessary changes. *To hell with this!* Institutionalization is sick. Too many Aprils, Christmases, Super Bowls and special anniversaries have been lost and forgotten in here.

An intrinsic certainty is a fact that once inquisitive inmates come up with their inferences about my two-day sentence they will begin to play dirty innocent jokes with covert intentions at serious bouts, a high percentage potential to result injured, or to catch additional jail time—oftentimes for someone else's misconduct. Thereby ignored their crazed gazes, and pretended being one hardcore criminal lest they tear my inner peace apart for their illicit incited pranks as everyone acts out a zombie look. A smiley face that my friends were accustomed to, done. Chummy short-timers are scales for their feasts.

We rode about three hours through main streets and busy boulevards, now with back-and-forth swings, alas; we know that our bus is inside of their premises' parking presidio. Outside, hoarse voices of troopers in cheerful laughter and diesel vibrations of two busses pulling up beside us.

By means of peepholes and mil-metric gaps in-between windows and deteriorated metals, we saw our second pistol-ready trooper as he descended and walked to the Inmate Reception Center, IRC, and stood in front of a tinted window, inserted our court transcripts into an underneath drawer, and saluted an invisible person inside.

As we waited, our driver aligned the bus about four feet away from an immense steel door that withheld a white label with bold red letters, "ABSOLUTELY NO WEAPONS BEYOND THIS POINT!" We unloaded as the end of our slightest opportunity to escape faded—and behind us, a sun-filled blue sky befogged as its door slammed shut.

FISHTANK FEVER

Four-men-per-wrist-chain, we descended our bus with verbal consent to walk two steps at once. Nearly thirty of us embarked into the Twin Titans' Main Entrance as a deputy yelled at one of its many reflective windows—"Fish!"—and two heavy steel doors extended inward and hummed as sacrificial tombs in Indiana Jones adventure films. An emergent gush of muggy air enwrapped us—it thrusted us backwards as when opening a steam cooker. As if we pushed its wind backwards, we stepped into a bottleneck hall with guides of blue, yellow, purple, green and red adhesive strips that lined its floor, which are marks that lead us further inside into different areas. For example, yellow leads to its hospital, green to our trustees, red for its release area and so forth.

A figurative red carpet introducing streetwise superstars from every undiscovered corner of Los Diablos County. Day and night; year round; nonstop. Paralyzed in here, sometimes one tries futilely hard to connect these familiar faces to someone we had probably seen stuck on the 405 or 110 freeways after we stereotyped ourselves in accord to our languages, ethnicity, prison experience and music choices.

Our fishtank's electrical door thrummed backwards and

sealed every outside commotion and this sparked a ghoulish reality and scary possibility to never exit again, alive. Our odds-and-ends are tricky. As we rode over here, someone in our bus's rear improvised a rap song with lyrics of, "There's no hell like our county jail my life is ended without a bail— we're jailed b-cuzz we bailed!—*Woopty!—Woo!*"

Once we stood inside, a marshal counted us, "Two! Four! Six!" then hollered aimlessly to our roof, "Thirty-eight!—Close fish!" Soon after, another door ahead of us buzzed open and a pack of marshals rushed us into our next module. Never two doors opened at once and without a direct command, signal, or a fisted knuckle on a window by an officer. Our stacked around concrete bricks, soundproof windows and luminous bulbs highlighted every deformity on our bodies and made our limbs transparent.

So far, most of us reached this new area, yet anyone of us may bawl, curse, collapse or hit our heads on its Plexiglas but to no avail; our watchperson on its opposite side ignores what happens in here, mostly. It is best not to behave erratic and uncivilized as this will offset nearby officers and they will step in only to drag *the problem* to a different cell for a quick toss-up; this present-day technological aquarium will transform any aquatic specie into a rainbow trout, a neon tetra or a fluorescent fish in a squirt.

Nearby, two reception marshals skimmed our pile of court papers as two deputies began to remove our chains and motioned everyone to sit on its floor; arms pulling both knees to our chins. Most of us found relief from our purple scars caused by cuffs choking our wrists as it seems that our indents will remain for a couple of days.

Every desperate new arrival that entered was in quick

search of a place to sit, crouch or to stand next to us, and this provides a psychological struggle in a progressive perilous stance. Some of these men do not enjoy anyone's look and may turn violent unexpectedly and unprovoked. As of now, some of us are in here for unknown criminal offenses, or until we hear it from a law guardian. Although serial killers, pedophiles, juveniles and wealthy men, among a bunch of slick predators, have an exceptional and separate booking procedure, a strong sensation lingers that not everyone is honest about their reason of capture.

They say that by its own mouth a fish goes into a fryer; likewise, our underwater pressure is tremendous, treacherous, and troubled. To contrive a mindset of a vigilante and of valor is worthy of a deceptive view. No one relaxed. Our stubborn motto: Trust No One.

A steady stream of cold air flowed out of its vents; it made my bladder swell and ready to spurt, but no urinal anywhere. A toilette's absence explains a skunky odor that penetrates our lungs and it made two fellows vomit in a corner. A drain duct on its floor's center *is* to urinate when not observed by a jailer; formalities had stayed outside. Inside of this tank is a two-way speaker inserted on a wall socket to communicate proposals—if someone would answer it— and besides, it is probably out-of-order and any attempts for sanitary concerns are void on its opposite end. Consequently, in extreme responses, dudes kneel down and unleash their rivers.

In a short time, everyone is un-cuffed and dandy, so upon our marshals' exit, my turn to pee. Security cameras installed in every hold-tank are primarily to survey criminal activities and probably not to spy leaking fish.

Castrated sea creatures—big and small—fresh and dirty fish whirled in, our space shrunk and crumpled as in a golden can of luscious caviar. No man has ever said that in-prison existence is leisure. This tanks' capacity label is marked for forty persons yet over fifty of us remain clogged in here. Somehow, a couple of hobos found a little space on its floor and nap.

Naturally, consumed, trapped, starved for food, cerebrally stupefied and an uptight need to outcry my inner child's lungs out in desperate shock yet forced back by our dark bulletproof glass and inescapable fort that surrounds us. Any verbal or physical message attempt is to ask for a severe shove or a toss-up by officers or inmates. Our seas' stillness and its overflow inundated our thoughts and abilities to move freely; no fish is safe.

This human receptacle is also known as "gambler's glasshouse" when specific syndicates of politicians, civilians, scientists and tuxedo businessmen tour it accompanied by law enforcement officials and investigators from various arrest agencies within Califa's justiciaries—and marshals from every state. Weekday business hours, they visit us and, in stealth mode, tip-toe and invisibly sway on its opposite side of its one-way mirror, sidled, yielded and indifferently peeped inside at us, like a pet shop walk. A wobbled civilized waterless aquarium, a reservoir of society's maladjusted, where men are crammed for explorers' tours of special-interest groups—*See-World!*

FISHY TAILS

Anew, filthy fish reeled inside. Amidst this flow of men, a surprised familiar face walked in, a black fellow in his upper-thirties appearing confident and brave, talkative and combative, gritty. Steadfast, we looked into our eyes, face-off mode, until we backed away and broke our rivers' silent stream.

My head tilted, "Wheres I know you from man?"

Thoughtful, he replied, "Yeeah! I-know-I-seen-you somewhere inside this muthafreaken' joints."

Trying to remember, "You evers been up-state?"

He smirked and said, "Psst! Holmes. Been checkin' in-and-out of this locked-up ghetto for a while. Seesaw, Rhino, Ironfist, *Wythe*!"

A ghostly joy pinched my soul but held those heartbeats in check and deceptively sounded hard, replied, "Yeah, that's it, Wythe, Cheeklewallah—Chucky's Crib!"

Astutely he agreed and continued, "Yeeah! What level wuz you up there in?"

My thoughts constructed a rare quick response—for it was thirteen years ago—"Nevada. Level twos, Bee-Yard."

Surely, we had drifted these undercover oceans a long time. Additionally, at this stage of petty preambles, no one is self-assured or contrite to reveal too much personal clues or penitentiary journeys in view that some of us are prizes for different shadowy objectives such as whistle-blowers, embezzlers and disloyalty, among other penitentiary code violations. Snitches on stitches is a well-known yard label and one that our majority abstains to even collaborate on it. Also, to cross our racial barrier is to defile jailhouse dogma and, instead, by fate, we conversed, with luck, against our unscrupulous odds.

Elated, he slurred, "Yeeahh! I wuz up there—'round ninety-one wheen it wuz brand neew." Simultaneously we discerned his whereabouts and with a mocked anger, replied, "Fuckin' lonely desert man!—Sandstorms, scorpions, tarantulas and some weird bullshit in that muthah."

Disheartened, he added, "Yiahh man, I paroled out of there 'round ninety-two and been in-and-out this muthah since."

Gasped and sad-hearted, said, "Shit. You tellin' me. We're both screwed in this boat"

Out of curiosity, he said, "So whut youz in heere foe now?"

Dishonest, replied, "Bunch of old tickets man, they just piled up and now I'm in here not even sure what some of those are for."

"Argh! You ain't lookin' at that much time. They got me on a darn violation, just hangin' around with my homiez. *Man!* I wuzn't even livin' out here—they picked me up in—*Riverside!*"

Shocked of that far-away county, maintained his interrogative onslaught limited, and off me, yet imbued our talkfest, "Damm! What you doin' way up nourth?

Remorseful and pitied, he said, "Man, I wuz doin' good over there. Had mah-bitch takin' care of me an'all I wuz doin' wuz hangin' at our hood's park with my homiez—you-knows-whut-I-mean! I guess a fool kain't even be out there actin's-a-clown—*period!*"

Frustrated, falsely agreed and added, "Forget these punks! They get you for any little crap. And if you ain't duin' nuthin' outside you might as well be jerkin'-off in here."

Relieved though still heated, he exclaimed, "*Foe-Sho!* Nigga kain't do this n kain't do that—I mean—niggas gotta have beats outside this shithole!"

Our arrests' coincidence amongst a bunch of strangers is speculative; to breathe someone's unwarranted brutality horrifies. My titillate mindset is that everyone is attentive for clues to discover deficiencies and make stereotypical and markedly, sometimes flawed, judgments through befriending talks. Predators of different types finely analyze, scrutinize—and divulge every uttered word. As ocean sharks track a speck of blood from miles away, so too, these men ones' weaknesses.

A relative irksome factor: this facility's loudspeakers persistent and varied inquiries, though more prominent is a round-the-clock query for deputies interested in overtime hours. Combined with our burst of anarchic chatter mixed with their compulsive disseminations turned our concert into a lock-tight psychic tumult. Quickly, amidst thunderous police codes and flea market verboseness came oft speaker-searches for unaccounted inmates with names such as John Doe, Harry Houdini and Freeway Freddy, and urged that whomever they may be to report to a nearby officer—whom are everywhere.

From now on, one begins to forget about our day's hour for until now we are timeless and, besides, who cares? We construe an approximate hour from whereabouts since we exited courthouses, our bus ride here and when we arrived at its parking lot, or we asked our new fish that entered "how it looks outside?" Creating dialogue just to entertain idle minutes. If ever one needs to think outside of a box or practice an elevator pitch or a circus blurb, this is it. "Globe's Greatest Gaff: U c us now; Later u won't." Nonetheless, to overly think or practice too much nonsense outside of this box may also condemn us again—by *our* judicial box, in an already condemned abyss.

Eternity encroached us. Hours passed—or that is what it seemed like, and we still have not moved. An increased smell of stale sweat, gutter, urine and unfamiliar dazed odors began to make us irritated then one fish lays a soundless rancid airy egg, it horrified us in-so-much-that someone blurted, "That ain't gas-tronomy homies. That's es-eych-i-tee!" Our high-flying sole had to squeeze his cheese in a noiseless whizz because excessive farts or vulgar displays may be valid reasons for verbal and physical aggressions by inmates of his own ethnicity. Flatus sufferers beware because in our fishtank, it is not a handicap but a gas station ready to blow-up.

As more fish enter, some of us are erratic, uneasy, and with our increased heat, some of our fish act as if they withhold first-degree burns, volatile. And nearly alike is a mob of mission oriented yet indolent three-strikers; incorrigibles, untouchables, eternals, and they will not fin anywhere or anytime soon therefore to stay out of their path is wise since they have little to lose. Our inglorious militarized homies; our lifers.

Configured within this array of fish are men agonizing from various forms of drug-abuse and start to demonstrate debilitating withdraw and brain disorders such as paranoia, tremors and seizures and, commonly, are verbally mistreated or even beaten by deputies or inmates.

A collective infusion of an infinite brand of social backgrounds and nationalities jammed and flocked in here creating a substantial overload; a claustrophobic heave. Men that come from different lifestyles and suburbs: Hollyweed, Belle Jardins, Komptone, Wreseda, San Fur and San Miguel Valleys, and annexed sections of Los Diablos County. Every ruffian is present: pimps, transvestites, wife-beaters, child molesters, rapists, fraudsters, blue-collar and new, though-not-so-well-improved cyberspace hackers.

An isolated categorized passage is for our troubled unusual suspects, infamous celebrities, for example— Beverly Hill's Fernandez brothers, Möntey Crew's Jimmy Lee, actor Bob Blacke and wealthy socialites and dignitaries. For their safety, these accused do not enter our fishtank's draggy process because they are prizes for start-up and low-rung criminals with an appetite for upward mobility within our lunatic penitentiary ladder.

In addition, we have psychiatric persons alleging no awareness of their crimes because they are under outside care of schizophrenia and Alzheimer specialists. Some of these fish are delusive and undergoing serious psychiatric bugs, still, in due time they must stand before a chancellor to answer a fundamental catechism, "How do you plead, guilty, not guilty, no contester?" and then atone for his or her answer. They too surely fit a medical malpractice, an unresolved mystery, or a Twilight Zone crime scene.

To illustrate, one of these fish tried to explain to any one of us who would listen and believe his story that, around two a.m.—just a little while ago, he gave "this woman" a ride to her home and as they drove and talked about their lives, she began fondling and licking his marbles. Now— his criminal charges include indecent exposure, lewd act, solicitation of a prostitute, driving with an expired license and tags, under the influence of a controlled substance and possession of a meth pipe and alimony default and lying to a peace officer and…. Notwithstanding any arrest warrants for unpaid tickets that may be stacked up in Los Diablos' Records Bureau. He too fits a depraved crime scene.

Within our midst of men, a few racketeers and extortionists philosophized their innocence by way of numbers, in that, a meaningless amount of cash taken from their swindles, their least amount of prison time, if any. In a sincere tone, they depict our model law-abiding citizen. These clean-cut and well-dressed competent money-launderers speak in a sophisticated language among themselves and sound so honest that their alluring schemes are hard to skip. And they often find a partner of interest in here to encourage and perform projects together upon their possible releases, an entrepreneurship of sorts. They too already fit an unresolved white-collar crime scene: premeditation to commit larceny.

Anyhow, a league of brawny marshals threw at us an enormous black homeless man who wore torn filthy clothes and so much coverture that his face is deficiently visible. He is weather-beaten: thick, aged scars on his cheeks, a tangled beard hangs to his chest, and a deranged hairstyle that makes him itchy as he pokes at it as if catching lice. This man is decayed and barefoot, and even though he seems aware of his jutted foul stench because his nostrils, like an ignited carburetor's lid, open wide in-so-much-that one can see inside at its years of hairy mucous clog open and shut as tight as a bi-valve. He does not say a word while he stands amidst everyone. His discolored grey iris and pupil of his right eye sags to its left corner of its socket as he gazes in cross-directions simultaneously.

Meanwhile, two white dudes crawled in and exposed red and purplish swollen faces wrapped around elastic bandages as they murmured a high-speed get-away chase against a caravan of patrol cars that ended in a suicidal wreck. Our jail's nurses provided their *best* unsuccessful effort to cover these men's cuts and bruises but their wounds are too many to hide. A third dude of their same peer limped in afterwards; a k-nine unit mauled him and now looks like a stitched puzzle. Added to their dogs' attack is this exemplary thrashing he received by a hive of upset officers. We sit together as he remains quiet and immobile; to convert into his shoes is unimaginable.

Coincidence or not, an irony between superiority and inferiority is always pressed in our fishtank and into our minds, sharks swallowing sprats. A bottom-line intimation of unequivocal expected etiquette from each stereotype. Our choked voices.

As toads in a puddle, we wiggle inside. At an hourglass's sandy pace, it could be somewhere around three or four at dusk—based on one inmate who glanced at a deputy's watch. It appears as though our intake jailers will process us further only until we complete a full house, or until they feel like it. Right now, we near sixty bodies.

One door screeched open and five young beefy white jailers cleared their way while slipping latex hand gloves and joking amongst themselves as a barrage of instructions directed us into a bigger tank. Their poster-look military haircuts, muscular and inflexible physical form made obvious their relative career tenure, rookies. As this group of uniformed men entered our tank of about forty-eight square feet, in a disarray clap of hands changed their laughter into a no-bullcrap demeanor, attitude, and nomenclature.

Marshal Luna, their lead spokesperson, thundered, "Everyone shut-up! Walk around the room in a straight line, left shoulders against the wall and keep your hands in your pockets." As if just out of bed, we formed a crooked line yet everyone silenced; chuckles exclusive for officers.

"Bump it up, dick to ass, shoulder to shoulder, no gaps in between! Anyone who does not cooperate gets everyone sent back!"

He slams again, "Do not look at me, my badge is holy! Do not pass gas, and do not talk to me! Just make a turn and look at the mirror in front of you!" At least a decent attempt to traduce his drills to Spanish, briskly added, "Entendei— 'migos! No passoe gassoe, no hablah inglish and no mirrow un polizio!"

Now, as we realize cultural strata appear as a preferred idiom, empathy non-existent, and racial profile symbolizes superiority, combined turned this conglomerate more intricate and critical for survival. Intelligence, questionable; race, unquestionable. Our tactic is to tailgate any fish ahead as we listen to their righteous commands; if not, any inmate caught goofing will end tossed onto its floor and kicked for not apprehending simple instructions. In our actual heedless mistakes adds to their strenuous objectives over their routine schedules and this is not smart from our behalf. They are not in here to bust a sweat.

Furthermore, at a certain particular stage, someone would raise his hand to indicate a missed sentence, or anyone who gargled, and as if by instinct, a mass of marshals quickly forayed removing this man to an empty cell to wait for our next timeless forward act. "Hey knuckleheads, listen-up! I ain't dealin' with your dumb-asses right now—m-o-o-ve when I say to move and s-i-t when I say sit!" He cries out, "I will hear myself in this module. My word *is* your wife. If I catch you talkin' or spyin' everyone stays here!"

Within our clan, we also have aged and impaired men alongside individuals with perceptive disabilities, antagonists and revilers, or so they say. A number of them are exfoliating prescriptive—and illegal—drugs' dormant withdraw symptoms; these men were more susceptive to harsh encounters by offensive villains. An underlined message is to adjust quickly, or be stuck in our fishtank's stench for an excruciating amount of time, to some men, even days.

Withal due diligence, jail is jail. However, our snarled faces and caprices from a galore of backgrounds, cultural, ethnic, character defects, social classes and moral deficiencies makes it certain that one man will screw *their* threats against our group's cohesive goal. Hushed and our foreheads inclined onto a thick glass divider when suddenly another deputy yells, "Take your clothes off except your socks and lay'em—do not throw'em—on the red line underneath you!

Keep your nose on that window at all times and close your eyes! If I catch you with your neck turned everyone is sent back!"

About five marshals stood dispersed at strategic points within our tank, nearly five more marshals supervised us for any slight twitch as they scattered and treaded our wallets, phone books, and miscellaneous items on its floor. We lean still against its soundproof tinted glass, buck-naked, man-to-man, and aloof listened to their churned and thorough toss-up of our belongings. Our fishy forum's temperature is around twenty degrees Celsius, safe to hold fresh meat cold, to avoid microbes and eliminate harmful bacteria, and to maintain a cool head.

Abruptly, a different deputy yells, "This is my favorite command for quick in-between-your-buns contraband check-up guys. Squat! Cough! An' spread'em!" In demonstrative disgrace, speechless, both hands grabbing our buns, motionless, held them apart and forever proved our universal hypothesis that man does not exist equally.

Marshal Luna stepped out and away from his giggling colleagues and yelled his next scripted brief command, "Pick up all of your shit! And, see that blue line under your feet, very well, step on it and follow it until I tell you to stop."

We trickled and simultaneously juggled our belongings into a long rectangular module with a strong chlorine or ammonia aroma though it was not a swimming pool. This one had about forty showerheads and faucet knobs circling it and as we jostled inside, he shouted again, "Stop right there! Do not turn it on until I tell you so. You have two minutes to get your ass cleaned up then flow into the next tank. Do it!"

Instantly, a few intermittent nozzles started to gush and

splash water onto a few naked bodies, as another deputy hollered, "Don't worry about bein' thrifty because it's paid for—by your granny, your sister or your uncle—or whomever is at home payin' *our* taxation—so dig in there and give it all you got!"

Some fish enjoyed their feel of cold water, some feinted to shower, and a bunch of us sidled onto our next cell. At their sight of dry persons, another marshal that also conducted, curtly scoffed, "Men! Water is free and you all know this ain't your Holiday Inn!"

Meanwhile, two trustees pulled two crates full of bundled county blues and two more crates full of lunch sacks and hurriedly lunged them as we rushed out of our showers. These paper bags contain a peanut butter sandwich, an apple, and grape juice. Flustered and no time to sit and eat, we nibbled it as some of us squirmed to remove our excess water. Eventually, everyone dressed and moved into a physical exam bureau and for racial segregation, fingerprints and identification to receive our booking bracelets and to have our dreadful mugshot snapped.

Afterwards, a keen team of nurses awaited us for x-ray imaging—and to ask us about hepatitis, tuberculosis, AIDS, and of our possibility of being a carrier of any transferable disease. Our interview ended as fast as we entered as they sounded patient even with a hinted attitude that they too begged for our prompt exit. They appeared bored and not overly concerned to proactive care for a bunch of demented men, as they will receive a nice paycheck either way. Nonetheless, some of us understood our nurses' cautionary intuitiveness, as only they know what type of incidents have happened in here before we arrived.

Amid reason of this ghastly madness, one slowly begins to regret every self-made mistake from our failure to comply in our societal structure of normalcy. A luxurious impeccable hierarchy that we will never achieve—as consequence of a misdemeanor or non-violent felony conviction. A forty-eight hour jail sentence as this intake process may last anywhere from one to seven days before we reach an assigned bed, if any, is ludicrous. A prolonged manufacture of our insanity pressed by a crawled loss of hope, dignity, and to deteriorate morals.

Moreover, our probability to encounter a verbal or violent dispute with a straitjacket on psychotropic drugs, or "*looney-tunes*"—their in-house label, thus to catch a new crime with an added sentence is always present. One false step or even a friendly smile and a simple handshake can go terribly wrong without a provoked cause with anyone as this ordeal unfolds and because men are prone to insecurities, anger and trifles. Jailhouse fights, riots and lockdowns are frequent, dangerous and unannounced; this premeditated mind-boggle and subversive stimulus is a subliminal dissipation of our self-esteem, prestige, spirit and love: Dehumanize.

Our ultimate goal within this techno-fortress is to reach a trustee dormitory, an empty dayroom or a stuffy tier, a bunk bed and recline. With so little time on my mind and a tangible Release Docket's printed receipt and its relay by way of an infinitude of intercoms is nerve-racking. In front of us are a few stainless-steel benches, concrete floors and stalls to relax our aching backs. Main-line inmates are too distant and unrealistic to reach them; our navigation is tedious and stressful.

Survival of our fishtank's process is not explanatory. Therefrom, when our nineteen-year-old homie did a one-year stint in this same county jail and then arriving to our hood, undiscerned, he asked, "Why is everyone moving so fast?"

JUVIE JUMBLE

"Every man's work, whether it be
literature or music or pictures
or architect or anything else, is always
a portrait of himself."
—*Samuel Butler (1835-1902)*[*]

How our society functions? Our RSVP was for a one-night symposium of up-and-coming artists at a new local museum—a previous shoe factory warehouse that still smelled of leather, glue, and cartons. At its loading dock, a banquet of champagne, wine, soda pops and recyclable water bottles among assorted cheeses atop crackers next to a variety of voluptuous *hors d'oeuvres.* Beside it, fancy plastic forks and spoons, pretty Styrofoam plates and cups. And just before we climbed a few stacked crates to enter our feast, two young female graphic design students who volunteered as receptionists waved visitors inside with soft, exotic and engaged hotline voices, "Welcome, indulge yourselves."

Couples of twos and fours careened inside, joyously entertained about, each group acknowledged their presence and chitchatted introductory phrases. Some of us, after four or five cheers, complimentarily aggrandized everyone's impressive oil and water canvas, earthy feet—human and animal—and silicone abdomen molds and clay head sculptures of recognized celebrities. A show-off of outstretched photographic exposures of famed scientific men and women, brooches detailed their inventive workmanships. From its dome descended braided artistic and asymmetrical decoupage cones; and on white doilies atop empty buckets were greasy lawnmower and auto parts and *Huntz*, *Nestle*, and *Similac* cans. Furthermore, decorative exhibits of handmade artisanal jewelry and earthenware lay in lowly strategic spots, on its floor, and on hooks.

Independently, and long before this gala, along with my youth friends we encountered deviant graffiti at grade education and through our high school's locker hallways and near our streets as it besieged our neighborhood's garage doors, parking lots, on abandoned stripped vehicles and hazardous alleys. Our communal laundry-room, "the spot", remained frequented by older teens, who hid in there to smoke *indica* and to form collages of colorful aversive Disney caricatures.

Every month at rent time, a few tenants would vigorously complain to our three-story apartment manager about its plumy cloudiness' earthy aroma thereof in gradual float and freely invading its lobbies though they never received any sincere outcomes. It appeared as if our leftover neighbors were unfazed by their indica's woody fragrance. Nonetheless, at this age, some of my all-around friends, whom also resided within, proudly showed-off black and white pins with "Just Say No" premonitions.

Our schoolbooks of our day—rock-n-roll and lowrider periodicals, trivial rags and *Homie's* flashcards combined an unraveled subway under-culture with its fashion clothes that kept us connected and dressed in street art thus we naively infringed societal norms. Among our trove were flaps of our *East Side Story's* classic oldies collectibles, bomber jackets, and *Breakdancing's* transfer from its vibrant disco floors onto our *hoodlum* riddled sidewalks and picturesque highway under-crossings filled with neon-like multicolored graffiti, as it was one of many fads of our day.

Still within our quarters, a round-the-clock passageway of men and women who had just moved into our complex, and a pack of attached pedestrians who did not live among us, possessed thug art tattooed sleeved down their necks, shoulders and arms. Most of our newcomers—we would later unearth, were evictees from nearby flats, were sought-after by far-off police agencies, and its majority were vigorous, perceptive, and muscular because of their recent releases from various penitentiaries. "We're on parole kids," they drabbed, "so go home with your mommy."

Among those parolees was an old scrawny creeper with a long forehead, slick-back hairdo, a thin hanged goatee and on his forearm, a cartoon tattoo of a muscled, tailed red devil and with a grin raised a pitchfork and when this villain showed it to us, he puffed, "an' tell'er that you just met Sir-Satan."

On a certain occasion, one of these ex-cons spray-painted a mural-size old-English *Noxs-Town!* on a main boulevard Mexican grocery store where passers-by saw it, some amused, most grudged. As I remember, no one dared to dial our police gang force on him, as it seemed possible that individuals reasoned to hold him as a known gangster instead of a neighborly enemy.

At just above ten years of age, some of us began to commit Robin Hood stuff, as a kleptomaniac urge and naïve pranks, which we later found that, were illegal when we soon found ourselves squatted on a curb beside a patrol car while detectives investigated us. Every so often, they took us for a *ride* to their headquarters even as for us it only instilled added curiosity into our discovery of weird outlaw scribbles that represented mobs, sex, violence, and derogatory messages: Éf da police! Éf—U-n-yur-hood, éf—this-n-that, and éffh—every-thang!

In addition, as we glimpsed under its worn mattresses, always found monikers of rival members and it frightened some of us to ponder that one day we might sit in here together—*and then what?* Bored yet our obsessive compulsiveness kept us busy as we moved and searched around for anything to contemplate—a staple, paper clip or a loose screw. Of course, under its rusted steel bed's frame were people's initials and squiggles of various hoods and engraved telephone numbers or an address to a social enterprise. Scratched on its door's tiny windows were various facial motifs; a premier view of our emoticons we use for e-mails today.

Inside of cells, various zodiac innuendos carefully scribed and elaborate scrabbles that came from raw materials provided by our jailers—such as toothpaste or deodorants—then we rubbed ink powder off newspapers and milk cartons then mixing those together to obtain *Play-Doh-like* globs of different textures and colors. Underneath of our top bunks we would daze at pasted magazine strips that formed montages some-of-which kept our minds occupied. As time transpired, we lied back and stared at our roof, oftentimes, its bright light bulb represented our sun for it always stayed on, and at night, our moon when it dimmed—thank heaven, a safety net of sorts whereas outside we risked our lives on our warlike drive-byes and bullet-infested streets.

A few detectives, as they filed their reports, we took an opportunity to roam and meet branch specialists, homicides, burglary, weapons and narcotics yet on top of their desks and within their cubicles hung curious prison-made gadgets and graphics stapled together. Our civilian-clothed agents said that these were hand-drawn relics from our hooligans whom they had sent to prison. They would show-off penitentiary artwork of happy and sad masks, amused and dejected clowns and smiley and sobbing [1]*Cholas*.

Also, among its array of black-and-white designs were detailed vintage vehicles such as Impalas, Monte Carlos', Buick Regals and a few classic mob-type roadsters. Polaroid prints of dudes stylistically leaned back with one leg in front and both hands inside of their parachute pants' pockets thrusting forward, [2]*Pachuco* trendiness—but in their backgrounds, serpentine barbwires atop brick walls and beside it a logotype of a marihuana penta-stem. These images of our culture's joyful and painful celebrations also contained neat handwritten titles that corroborated with varied genre songs such as "Jailhouse Rock", "Folsom Prison Blues", and "Another Brick on the Wall". This form of interpretive art was named, *Ink From Our Pens*, and our journals, *Pen Pals*, long lost.

---

[1] Cholas: a teenage girl who associates closely with a gang of cholos (thugs) or is a cholo's girlfriend.

[2] Pachuco: a young Mexican living in the U.S., esp. one of low social status who belongs to a street gang.

Among our street art collectibles were descriptive folklores of [3]*Charras*, [4]*Aztecas*, [5]*Pancho Villa*, and folders filled with illustrative cultural and revolutionary Mexican legends. Multicolored mystic pyramids, mazes of ancient empires, and a variety of mythological symbols that captivated our artists' curiosity and creativity—who were current and ex-prisoners. Well, we assumed that if an imprisoned *homie* did not have a legit address—as some of us were illegal aliens—to forward his sketches to, he would mail it to his detectives' name as our only known and useful address was of our sheriff's station: 4321 Knox Boulevard.

Albeit, our artist was not an artist, he was a homeboy we knew within our streets. Although most of those souvenirs represented our gang's counterculture paraphernalia—and unconcerned for societal norms, nevertheless, why these rebellious manifestations not in their precincts' evidence room? In courtrooms' archives? In its rightful owners' home? Every detail is lost when not set in copyright or patented forthwith.

At a predetermined schedule, a couple of detectives transferred us to their corresponding courthouse's underground detention and our squiggles on walls and doors continued with its similar approach yet now enlarged figures of women, drugs, gangs, and anti-social political remarks. Every image connoted its unique and interpretative view to

---

[3] Charras *(pl)*: a Mexican female equestrian or cowgirl, typical of one wearing an elaborate outfit, often with silver or gold   decorations, of tight trousers, ruffled shirt, short jacket, and sombrero.
[4] Aztecs *(pl)*: a member of a Nahuatl-speaking state in central Mexico that was conquered by H. Cortés in 1521.
[5] Pancho Villa: Francisco Doroteo Arango *"Pancho"* Villa, 1877-1923, a Mexican general and revolutionist.

everyone locked inside. At this age and time, we knew that to destroy federal property was vandalism and punished by added jail time and/or fines. We did not care.

Back in 1987, at Los Padrotes Youth Hall in East Los Diablos County, our admonishing came immediate and firm in regards to their zero tolerance policy for every tag form: "You tag—you're it—you paint!" In here, nearly eighty of us amassed new ways to manufacture simple objects with imaginative mindfulness and our hands, manual arts. Religious and artisanal pendants constructed with clear wraps taken from our meal packages and pieces of leather and soft plastic ripped from torn seat covers of our transport squad cars.

About half of our boys seemed relaxed and in a mild state-of-mind when they started their self-start-up kits: they pulled and wrapped plastics into thin ropes of various sizes, then curled it, compressed it, and intertwined a variety of colors thus aimed it toward their objects' intended product, this depended on gathered materials, and its amount. Out of their destructiveness surged their creativeness that soon become evident: wool crosses, plastic necklaces, threaded ankle bracelets, leather wristbands and rings of every size and signatures attached.

We rounded up additional materials to knit as we frayed our uniforms and inner garments that conjured up different thread hues particularly Fruits of their Looms' reds, whites, and blues. However, this too was illegal to deface county property, a misdemeanor if less than a thousand bucks worth or a felony if a thousand and above. After a short pause, we pried our guard's presence followed by his absence and quickly restarted to form rainbow nametags made to individual taste and promos to exchange for jailhouse must-have items.

Anyhow, to destroy state or federal wardrobe was not my interest nor to sew thread adornments, rather, acquiescence of our original gangsters' intended wicked ideology, to back our [6]*vatos locos,* to party with our [7]*homegirls* and to joyride roundabout our streets in [8]*firme carruchas.* In spite of that, this too got us in trouble, as it was unlawful to loiter, behave disorderly, and late-night cruising.

Conversely, this apprehension was our perfect timespan to make contrasts about our lives and positive changes to our unruly behaviors. For instance, a precise excuse to relegate our spirits to *Christ* to redeem us from this wayward accident. Also, this was an opportune break to seek our cherished and *Blessed Virgin of Guadalupe* to plead for every harm we had caused society. Primarily, to make amends with our families, significant friends, and with ourselves.

Nonetheless, on our way to probe with new sketch techniques, it became useful to hold ourselves away from troublemakers. Besides, six months at Camp Snoopy, and many more, had taught us to draw cartoons, flowers, unicorns and toy cars. True, to illustrate contemporary art or any abstract form of it, one does not need to go to juvie, but it was part of our growth processes, our deceitful lowlife totem pole.

By the way, as early as juvie jail one may easily become a victim of ample problematic, disturbed, and physically stronger youths by their ingenious Machiavellian tactics,

---

[6] Vatos locos *(pl) (sl)*: crazy dudes.

[7] Homegirl(s): *Syn. Moll*; a gangster's girlfriend(s).

[8] Firme carruchas: fancy classic mobster vehicles.

perceptual slavery, or tattletale treachery. In retrospect, we remained thoughtful, concentrated, alert and cautious of every activity that happened near and around us, as it was critical to do so. Moreover, our discreetness not to overload ourselves with depressive attitudes or affected by tension or fright about our cagey sphere since to panic or show nervousness are signs of ones' weaknesses, hence, precarious.

PRISON ART

Undoubtedly, centuries ago, Plato foresaw our communicative techniques when he philosophized, "Mind is ever the ruler of the universe." Mine standard 6-by-8 square-feet of measured universe.

With time for self-reconciliation later and juvie in my memory bank; reached adulthood, age wise, even with an underdeveloped cerebral complex—or full maturity, as an increased outline of psychological and scientific probabilities had more open-ended questions than our universal hunger epidemic. "Is *it* in your genes? Do any of your family members suffer from *it*? When did *it* start? Does *it* have *its* own doctor?" Above ten years of analytical researches as an exhausted spin wheel rodent, their inconclusive data became palpable, "It's because you dropped out of high school moron!"

The experts would educate my beyond repair frontal lobe because its dopamine pathways, molecular receptors, and a voluntary clinical research found that neuron "A" that connects to "B" to "C" to "M" to "#@?"—exterminated! By illegal drugs. Next!

Bit by bit I began to abstract our homely humble upbringings' and core values as our association with our gang's loathsome shift increased its sinister ordeal and oft drug use diminishing our moral capabilities and soon was blindsided again and sitting behind bars at Los Diablos Men's Main Jail, best known as *the county* and *cee-jay*. Emotions withheld and time perceived as an uncompromising logical sequence of life though deep inside of me remained a tearful soul filled with loneliness and despair for having reached a reformatory harsher than juvie. Yale encapsulated jail. Tenth Floor, Denver Row, Cell Number Fifteen, exactly its bottom tier's middle.

A crazy man's castle, howbeit, we continued to improve our artistic portfolios and criminal recognitions—and more adverse for we are no longer received a slap on our hands for quirky misdeeds then tripping us for *Camp Snoopy's* for summer or winter ghetto getaways, grimacing.

Already inside of its barred door, glimpsing at its cell's form—as if to measure it to see if I would comfortably fit in it, to its far left corner of its flawless floor lay a tidy newspaper wastebasket. Furthermore, this oblong cave's decorative dullness were colorful springy birds, rollercoasters and copycat toys cleverly constructed from spare Thyme, Pupil, and International Geography magazines and arranged to resemble a *canny* adventure park. This brought back memories to some of us who at some time in our lives had visited any dreamlands' playground.

From D-Row's straightway, its cells' rectangular shapes appeared sufficiently comfy and resemble a boat's chamber or a train's cabin—excluding its luxuries or amenities, and once locked inside an opposite reaction takes over. Stepping into its equipped cement block, in delicate manner, which is aligned with permanent homely furnishings of different materials—steel and concrete—that reflect real *IQEA* appliances thus gave this studio an animated phony *welcome-in* invitation.

To illustrate, on our entrance floor an old pillowcase functions as dust mat and over our sink at face level is a square foggy piece of aluminum foil that helps to serve as a gimmicky mirror. In addition, a brown carton cylinder vase sits on a desk with a lucent flower inside of it. Unquestionably, our best of home economics by our averted previous boarder as he left a brief superposed memo on an unsubstantial, shaggy paper wreath, "Zailenze, Plí-zz!"

Further inside of this large-scale cellblock—resembling a high-rises' flank, daunted along toward my appointed unit congratulating every new mate and side-eyeing every handrails' gaps because a mishmash of men stood shirtless with their fully tattooed arms extended and swinging newspapers as they hollered high-fives since it is underground code to do likewise with every fish.

Some of my new crimees flapped Asian style fans as they refreshed their disinterested sarcastic joyous unemotional bearings. One inmate in particular, appeared to be our shot-caller, exchanged kites with someone else in an upper tier. In a raspy tone, he whispered, "Psst! Homie! Ay see yous, ay hear yous, ay feel yous but ay cain't reach out-n-touch yous. Howevah, ayes cain protects yous."

Besides our bunk kickbacks and not a whole lot to keep our hands busy or to prevent too much talk, some inmates demonstrated exotic talent through exhibits of doomy dungeons and dragons, furious serpents intertwined in cracked boney skulls, and angelic figures paired with demons. For the majority of us, every miscellaneous venture we had amounted back in juvie, this cee-jay higher education was to become our prowess of minutiae artistry. Although our items' appeals and bulk was primarily out of our slums, in contrast, there appeared splendid portraits of lifelike women and children and friendly families filled with love.

Some of these young men have not reached their legal age to purchase a pack of cigarettes yet are headed to gruesome adult prisons and once inside of any state corrective property, criminal institutionalization sprouts. More so, for those of us who hold criminal backgrounds, prior run-ins with law officials and judicial arrest warrants, thus, a combination of toxic elements lead our minds', spiritual and physical, hardened emotions within this oft supervised penal entourage of our paths. In this way, hordes of nationalities and social classes preserve our steel revolving doors intact.

Cops and homies, crime and punishment, jail and recidivism results are its bleak magnitude by how a minuscule percentage of us become aware—or dare to awaken our innate gifts toward positive synergy. To some of us, this established associative endeavor is an opportunity to discover our crafts and become proficient as we learn to express it constructively; our infinite ingenuity grows. Case in point, we cannot continue to break laws, commit more crimes, or violate parole or probationary mandates. We need not aide recidivism to our already prison crowdedness only to discover and/or increase our unique talents—as bigger and better art seminars abound for hand-to-eye coordinate instruction, visual language and stencil techniques. In addition, poetry programs and appalled playful puppets await nearby to practice and polish our nascent crafts.

CHUCKY'S CRAFT

Booh! I-t i-s not our horrible movie icon…

Pablo Picasso said, "We artists are indestructible; even in a prison, or in a concentration camp, I would be almighty in my own world of art, even if I had to paint my pictures with my wet tongue on the dusty floor of my cell."*

Everywhere, felons too, always invent new ways to manifest our thoughts and perceptive senses. Prison riots, many times, are consequences of our vaulted failures and mistakes topped with a protective belief of, as we say, *our principle*. On our adversary, this preconceived premise may be an everyday word or clause, a lollypop or a cigarette, breath or death.

We strive within society's penitentiary system with patience await our turns for whatever type of expressive vehicle may be granted us by its ruling circles. Therewith, our jail saying, "Nah! Nah! Nah! Homie. Don't wait for them to give you anything you just go out there and take it!" Meanwhile, gaining our casual due right for dignity—and in its process obtain our long-desired voice—in categorical regulative stages especially when some of us are truly innocent of our formal writs and court convictions. Despite our moral shortcomings to circumvent society, some of us contribute—and still adhere to prideful distinguished adaptations and rightful amends.

Nineteen-ninety, winter gone. Locked up in Cheeklewallah's Death Valley State Prison—Chucky's Crib, its secondary name—an interstellar comet passed-by. That year's frigid season arrived literally as a breeze and into our past, it went. Our acclimatized centerpiece of infernal waves of scorching heat that kept us bathed in sweat and preoccupied for six consecutive months.

This humongous concrete-and-iron compound sits amidst an immense desert that borders interstates Nevada and Califas and from a telescopic view appears as a minimal matrix withholding steel-melt temperatures. We fancied about an escape route as that was our best ballad to entertain us since we had plenty of time to think and sketch many stanzas—even if our pipe-dream is to cross an unmeasured Sahara without a water pouch or a guide's help to excavate immutable walls, floors, and roofs. Our alternate myth is that one future day we will get out of this stable and cross its dunes—as a heard of camels onto blooming pastures—at least while we kept our bodies in operational form with something—anything—everything worthwhile. A pencil, a pen, or a tattoo-machine.

At some time whilst intake, and just before we entered our mainline yard, a mandatory psychoanalysis of every new arrival by a decent doctor, probably a retiree or headed for Medicare, who did not make an attempt to look up as he dozed off while he surveyed an empty file and intermittently burped, "Blah-Blah! Er, it's okay—it's okay."

Ghastly snapped back up and said, "Do you suffer or

have you ever been diagnosed for autism or received any form of cognitive therapy?

A quick reply, "Yeah! Might be borderline psychotic. Not quite sure if I'm in or out."

Calm and suspicious turned and said, "You are *definitely* in."

With innocence looked at him, "Do I qualify to find work in here?"

Skeptical, he answered, "*Who* isn't qualified?"

Our psychiatrist lazily continued with his initial evaluative psychological template:

"What is your pet's name?"

"Necio."

"How old are you?"

"Nineteen sir."

"Where are you now?"

"Locked-up."

"Do you know your eternal serial number?"

"Yes! YA-65544."

"Do you have any enemies in our yard?"

"Well, no idea. Haven't entered our yard yet and don't know who lifts weights in there."

He added, "Does anyone know that you are here?"

"Huh!" And in a returned whisper, "What-the-hell?"

Both of us staple our confused stares across our gazes albeit with his amazed susurrate doctoral understanding, "Poor child."

He knew that a sandbag of puzzled interrogatives overflow his mind and may follow; however, a line of men waited behind, so he straightened his lenses and in apathetic demeanor looked at his stack of desk folders and nodded to end our one-minute interview, pulled its top file and faintly gasped, "Neggst!"

Boom! Lowriders luck: low-security level yard, a low bunk-bed, and a low-pay kitchen job. *Heel-low Cheeklewallah!* There is a job for everyone in jail.

Bee-Yard, medium security surveillance, a formidable administrative segregation system and an amused concoct of movie-like personalities. Amidst everyone alleviating our continuous ticktacks—those strolling our Olympic track, basketball or soccer players, weight lifters and pigeon feeders. *Chicali from Mexicali*, had a routine of searcheing for rocks of various shapes, colors and sizes and sneaked those inside of our dormitory for a project that he assimilated with *The Flintstone Era*. And for every fascinate curio added to his evolutionary idea, excitedly grinned ear-to-ear and squealed—*"Cheekle-wallah-yapa-zapa-dooo! Theel-maaa!"* His ex-wife that rewarded him two years for domestic violence.

As a pastime, he bonded those pebbles forming barns, volcanoes, castles, and creative wonderful natural landscapes followed by decorative solid bases with souvenirs that he would encounter buried in our sandy yard such as dead snakes, tarantulas, centipedes and scorpions' shells. Our climate's frequent sandstorms infused our yard with a variety of desert shrubbery, weird beetles and swarms of abnormal crawlers and weird insects in-so-much-that it was mandatory to remain alert whenever we inspected our linen and boots every sunrise and nightfall for any covered unsolicited poisonous terrestrial invaders. In truth, even within our twelve-foot murals we must abide with restrictive measures for Animals' Rights, "Beware of dangerous desert dwellers, they *may* be poisonous. Do not tease or capture them." In fewer words, in case of a rational face-off, do not hurt our creatures; immediately, *dial us, Animal Control.*

Chicali's hobby flourished into a business as soon as it caught other prisoners' inquisitive suspicions, for our greater good, dudes paid for his marvelous rocky products by way of cigarettes, soups, cosmetics, coffee and candies. Somehow, someway, our guards and blue-collar personnel also pre-ordered *to-go*, probably by transferring funds into his account. At that time, it was certain that those stunned handiworks' price were for once-in-a-prison-time masterpieces, perhaps. Moreover, its dexterous architectures bewildered everyone as those concepts left many of us to wonder, where is this foreign wild zoo? As a short-circuited and electrifying prisoner amplifies—"We're trapped in it!"

Anyway, almost any loose object that lies in here may be useful as someone will attain an ingenuous way to create any particular piece out of what seemed as junk whether for productive purposes, or otherwise. Proof of this is how some of us collect empty chip bags or cigarette cartons, and assembled colorful picture frames, utility boxes, crafty toy bicycles and skateboards then enwrapped those in cellophane to give them a demonstrative shiny display and a just-out-of-our-factory feel. *Ride, anyone?*

Our ultimate prison achievers are those whose labor gripped, intrigued and wowed. Portraits of beloved families and awesome paints of Nature and Wild, picturesque graphics of our infinite universe and its galaxies. Inventive cartoonists' sketches likewise astonished us. One of those caricatures was of ex-President Ronald Reagan as he blinked an eye while he puffed on a Cheech-and-Chong cig and in its background a Drugs Equal Alienation logo and this pieces' title in jet-smoke letters, "Just Tell Them Hell No!"

Our tattoo artists perplexed everyone with their trade more so when most of their tasks is without pre-drawn patterns, they continuously ink someone's body, that is, until our guards came near. Their business included creations of unique—tailor-made—diagrams that someone may aspire to have *ink-jected*.

Nonetheless, our time behind bars awakened us to a vivid spectacle that our downward spiral is deeper than once perceived from outside of it. Over time, as we march inward, it becomes darker and more frightful; our engrossed freedom of expression converts into an airtight, filtered, and hypocritical endeavor, as in Chucky's malevolent film plots.

We realize that raised street-smart is not a crime whereas a lifesaving evolution. With certainty, our fancy stories are plenty about our criminal gurus who made a quick dash such as Bonnie and Clyde, Al Capone, Pablo Escobar and infamous dangerous minds or unlike our spoils who did not get away with any stash and now sit here paying its price.

Furthermore, our marginalized and disfranchised status consequently leaves us in an uphill and almost endless battle to reincorporate mainstream society. An ironic maxim is that taxpayers pay its tab, fight crime and live long.

In general, hope is not lost. A shocking deterrent where besides being condemned two years for clumsiness, though not wholehearted shackled, quietly contributed. Our vitalities are critical to our bodies' resistance to imprisonment. It seemed like we traversed a fairy museum and navigated an adventurous lapse; checked-up and came to terms with yet a novel view of our ever-crude innards of prison artistry. Equally analyzed, then society in every way will believe that our truth is nothing more than these artifacts' shadows.

In conclusion—not seclusion, forlorn men, women, and juveniles clutched in this legislative systematic confined and institutionalized web deserve a bit of social support. We are aware that just as a dog is unleashed from its cage after a long time it is only to attack its own kind, so is man. A-n-d, hereupon is *how our society functions.*

> "Art is not a handicraft, it is the transmission
> of feeling the artist has experienced."
> —*Leo Tolstoy (1828-1910)*

THE MAN'S OFFICE

"Let freedom reign."—*Nelson Mandela (1919-2013)*[i]

Southside Califas, 10:00 P.M., last week of September 2009. Our beloved Los Diablos Badgers are playing at San Quinten's Candlestick Park an intense season's end tie ballgame against our archrival Jiants and a play-off berth at stake for either team. Top of the ninth inning, two outs and a runner is at second base in cat-and-mouse posture with the opposing pitcher.

Abruptly, our telephone unsuspected beeped and caused me to spill a cold beer out of my grip and onto our living room's rug. A private number appeared on its display as it interrupted my pastime, gave me a gig to do, and miss our game's most memorable play, on a peaceful autumn night. Very odd since my only Voice call is with a woman coordinator from Immigration's Special Supervisors who every weekday makes verbal contact before noon.

Skeptical, picked up its receiver, "H-e-l-low?"

A man with an assertive bass tone responds, "Hello! With Mister Garcia please!"

"Y-e-a-h, what's up?"

"This is Mister Stevens from I.S.S! We need you in our office first thing tomorrow alright."

"O-k-a-y? I will make it."

"Thank you. Please show up."

We courteously split greetings and affirmed our unconventional summon.

Receiver down, my deep hidden hindguts tightened as I became dubious—abstracting myself and sending our upcoming battles of October baseball fever straight into my mind's closet. Why an immediate demand to revisit them? On second thought, this agent sounded apprehensive and did not explain an exact reason for their firmness to arrive early tomorrow. What is their rush? What is their importance of difference between first or last errand tomorrow? No appointed time or contact person, or verification of any data that pertains to our buddy-up contract. Where are we heading with this swift visit? That is, in previous clandestine S.W.A.T. mode bust, they just came and battered our door down, then ransacked our house only to inquire about my whereabouts. Cruel Cupid loomed in tonight's chilled fog and a cold prison bed needs a warm body, I thought lightheaded.

This stoolie is another new Case Specialist that took over as my coordinator with Immigration and Naturalization, as he reassured, "Just report into our office tomorrow, don't bring anything with you, it's imperative that we see you." An indirect yet concise hidden memo: jail. What else might it be? Their lame trick was not smart; right now, fifty-two states await my arrival.

Two days ago, they asked for an in-person interview at their headquarters and our conference went routine, barren.

We had agreed to meet once every week and, of course, upon their untimely requests. Those visits deduced their primary business inside of a makeshift office, which is to document, and monitor hundreds of legal and illegal green-card holders, not American Express cards, through various federal hearings processes.

As if to smoke pot is better to my conscious because this round of telephone calls left my reason in incomplete comprehension of what they exactly sounded like, that is, they must see me in a slammer—*pronto!* And so tonight, a whole twelve-pack of beers will be gulped down my liver as it is calculated that no one guarantees a fresh one tomorrow.

More pathetic, a bright idea popped into my brain of a crucial choice either to surrender—as they inexplicitly asked, or to become a federal fugitive by skipping town. Should my surrender be a logical choice? This option will end my raucous escapisms, and to move and eat my food of preference; and my second guess will allow me some time to travel around our country, or flee it—but for how long? A critical compromise with a whole night to make up my mind.

At midnight, our television is still running infomercials and my beers are gone, our game is over.

Waking up early on a hazy daylight was a miracle and simply dressed to match jail's colors: a gray tee shirt, black tennis shoes and blue jeans plus a few bucks in its pockets. At a nearby corner from our home, a bus arrived with a black female driver, exchanged niceties and asked her for directions to a specific address inside of downtown Los Diablos County, after she listened politely confirmed that her route would drop me off right at the federal building's doorsteps. Without breakfast, my stomach knotted as I said, "Thank you, maybe we meet again on our way back." She gave me a courtesy smile, stepped on its pedal thus sent me to her bus's backend where a derelict man slept, and drove away and certainly, now appeared as an immigration agent disguised in a Metro Transit Association uniform.

In our guests area, a mid-thirties clean-cut Caucasian man in great physical form stood and did not fit our kinship of Latin heritage present and pestered us into *the mans' office*. A farcical character: An undercover agent? A set-up man? Our gatekeeper? My guillotiner? He spoke in an indiscriminate manner among our majority of Hispanics quietly appointed here, nervous, thoughtful and of worried composures awaiting to enter—as none of our previous men exited *the man's office*.

Again, that bright idea to sneak out of there a free man or just to start a possible unwarranted jail sentence was still up for grabs. As that thought ever-so-slowly processed, it turns out that our white man that chatted with us began to explain his adventurous journey from Poland to Hollyweed to start an actor's career though he began to irritate and sound bogus. As time crept us by, space to roam in our lobby waned and as more indigents arrived, it turned our corridor into a distress mess.

Amidst his nonstop jive, an Immigration and Naturalization agent opened a door, hollered a list of Spanish names and gestured us inside. Our European shut his mouth, and in sarcastic laughter, looked at us, raised his buttocks midair, forced a loud fart and shouted, "Hang-in-there *hah-migoes!*"

Trapped!

C.C.A'S WAYS

Life is curious, like 1980's Dream Team's basketball superstar Marvin "Magic" Manson used to dish up no-look passes to his teammates; likewise, serendipity swished and slam-dunked me. As freshmen, we sashayed inside of our high school cafeteria's vinyl floor accompanied by gorgeous teenage girls who smiled while we spontaneously held our plastic trays full of food. Suddenly, as if an impetuous deity maliciously underhanded that leather bean-ball at my face and, in consequence, twisted my neck three-hundred-and-sixty degrees to get a better view of our current news. Now, we stand inside of a prison mess hall amidst an elongated line of grumpy old detainees who also hold empty stainless steel trays outside of a blank counter's peephole.

Wednesday, this is my third day inside of Clearway Correctional Authorities somewhere within an ardent dune of a Mexican-American border, probably southernmost San Fuego District, Califas. Our barricade's security guards and most of its detainees sound alarmed and absorbed as if we just won the lottery for a great chunk of time in detention. *Heck no!* Home, family and friends await, by next week, perhaps.

Effectively, it feels awkward and leery *doing time*

without basic jailhouse programs such as yard-time, labor posts, letter writing or moral contingencies to keep oneself busy and upbeat. Otherwise, we just roam and doodle our same activities every day such as playing cards or dominoes, exercise or shadowbox, skim the same old science-fiction books and timeworn gardens and parents magazines since some of us only stare at repetitive flicks. Usage of their private handsets is overboard expensive to dial our contacts often. A plain miracle seems surreal inside of world's Call Center of America.

Locked inside of a two-bed cell, a priority is to always revise its mattress to remove any concealed contrabands that might be in it—such as drugs or weapons—that might belong to a previous man who slept on it or its present resident. Possession of cellphones by anyone is illegal, which includes our guards. Hence, our last problem is to have a hidden cellular beep at midnight by unknown shoppers. *Hell!* Someone wishes to check-in or buy crank.

As we sit alone in our dayroom, we watch and listen to some *real* prison-raised adults as they argue and confront our weak guards as impersonators of face-to-face WrestleMania duels. These baldhead fully tattooed beasts are only a few outspoken and offensive individuals whom always roar at our guards for a most miniscule mistake as if *we* are perfect although that bully attitude does not change our dim outcomes as their monotonous response is, "we are only doing our jobs."

Moreover, repeated altercations irritate staff members whom, in consequence, restrict our dayroom time and leisure activities as our guards feel disrespected and threatened. An immature mood that is anticipated and disappoints because most of us will be in here for an average of six months—it may be longer due to our court processes evolution, its litigious length, and case difficulty. We assume that every adult human must stand up for his or her own rights; in here, a most apprehensive behavior is our guards' lack of assertiveness for this module.

As of now, we have not encountered any major verbal disruptive or pushy conflicts that instigate violence amongst ourselves as our majority attend our own arm-length space, entertain our egos, and leave our next detainee at peace—and this is superb for our wellness. Impromptu lock-up combined with lonely and limited space to roam exasperates and creates storms of outbursts on some of us, it is expected role-play due to our excessive stillness and stress and hunger.

Additionally, any specific day-to-day adaptations or exercises take an extra effort as a direct result of *their* unrehearsed bait, which was from my home's comforts then a fast-forward scene into a jail cell. Whatever happened to *Due Process of Law?* Undue Process of Flaw? No *Miranda Rights* or even a free telephone call, indeed, we are their stooged screws of a broken immigration engine. Not one Washington agent has approached us to explain our maniacal barricade, our snatched freedoms. No good-byes to our loved family members, and no farewells to our lauded neighbors. If they would have ransacked my home during that last telephone talk and amidst that night's baseball game, our big screen set would still be on with Judge Judy, the Twilight Zone and Gilligan's Island.

Haphazardly, a bothersome inguinal hernia that is stuck between my testicles frustrates my workouts as certain poses and moves are more arduous. When we passed our welcome stage a few days ago, our doctor saw it and asked about my medical history and, without an analysis, sincerely prescribed plenty of rest as he added, "As long as it does not protrude or provide you a preponderate pinch, it is perfectly positioned in its proper pocket."

Furthermore, as if enrolled in a dental dispensary, an oral infected chip surfaced on a corroded lower molar; however, our varied illnesses receive their same indifferent diligence. No detainee will visit our dentist's office without first stricken by a bloody seizure attack.

Right now, everyone is in our dayroom, spread about in shameful silence—except for two boisterous televisions that throughout an entire day run helter-skelter nonstop Peah Pet, Hawk Glasses, and Huffington Ford's car auction infomercials. Our 10:00 A.M. count will start soon so we must return into our cells for their same ol'—same ol'. This temporary lodge is a metallic gray pentagonal pod with our guards' podium at a specific corner adjacent to a lone, red secured door and from it; he has a perfect viewpoint of its upper and bottom tiers' forty-eight units in opera theatre architecture.

My cellmate goes by his childhood nickname of Tree-Top, a Mongolian, who is also on their list of displaced aliens, and waits for his republic's regime to come and pick him up, or so he says. After he signed his *Voluntary Removal* contract, he has been on its *Hold List* for two weeks so now his exit is in suspense for an aerial flight back home. Nevertheless, a financial struggle developed, adding, that his country's kingdom will not pay his flight costs, and a patriotic standoff is their reiterated reluctance to accept American-raised felons. His Mongolian authorities do not accept unreformed, unreconciled and remorseless felons walking their vast floral gardens. He will make it home but they wish his release from here to Mongolia as a pedestrian so that they have time to make appropriate homecoming celebrations.

In spite of that, whom should we ask about his home dream to become reality? As our Judgment Day prophesy's date of arrival or our Parole Board to exonerate us, no one knows.

It appears as though his Mongolian authorities, through Inter-poulí-z, is aware of his seven years in a maximum-security oceanfront Seesaw Solitary State Ward for *attempted murder*. His top-notch cover-ups in many of Seesaw's insane foster care gory riots, two years spent in solitary housing units and a pile of reports of his verbal threats to injure jailhouse administrates. Besides, we need not worry about his psychological diagnosis as it sits in a neat pack and in a safe box in one of Califas Rehab Rangers' archives along with his psychiatric appraisal. This is what we know of, whereas, what about what we do not know of? Nevertheless, similarities attract, so from now on, we may become homies.

Among our numerous nationalities, we have an aged Caucasian hunchback from either Latvia, Yugoslavia, Moldavia or one of those long-dissolved Baltic States that present-day Russia does not officially recognize or if it even belongs to its European Union. Grandpa switches his story into riddled plots and turns. And this guys' fortune probably hangs on a satellite scope of geographical political conflict, in part, due to his proclaimed unknown ancestry or birthplace. At space-time gravitational speed, our old man is stuck in here until *further notice develops* from *any* country on its eastern hemisphere that will accept him. Ethnic wars and social uprisings in those countries do not help him much.

Anyhow, he says that it does not matter which country accepts him—he only begs to be out of here. His options are for Immigration and Naturalization—which holds us; a Human Traffic Squad—which he has a lawsuit; or a Traveller's Lodge Charter—which he cares less, to relocate him in a hometown *somewhere* in our cosmos, a sort of diplomatic accord. It is easier to pick a territory's name out of a magician's hat and then aid him into an unmarked airplane with plenty of fuel to go around our planet. We hope there is a take-off or landing strip outside.

Be it as it may, his process to repatriate, and, of state approval may take many years, *or forever*, as every legal procedure seems from inside of our five concrete barricades that mesmerize. And, whether he doggedly orchestrated these Supreme Court-caliber paper projectiles for his love of this food, or because our comfort zone is better than in a war-torn country, or because he has no more family members to look after or they after him, we will never uncover.

As evil overlooks us, he will celebrate his ninetieth birthday with a debut of a carrot jumpsuit inside of a cell with a sort-of-a frivolous yet camouflaged federal festivity framework to celebrate it amongst us, barring Martha Stewsart. He may also help himself if he halts a number of grievances he fired against prominent fixtures such as Immigration and Child Endowment, Clearway Correctional Authorities, the Center for Investigations Agency, and a few state and federal Appeals Courts. Some of these tribunal processes may carry-on for many months before those arrive to a judges' bench—or anyone's desk.

As of now, he has been in here two-and-a-half years and for every gripe commenced come added delays in his goal to repatriate, or exculpate, or escape. He believes that these civic agencies retaliate for his political speeches, of which we are unaware. This patriotic standoff makes him resemble a disgruntled veteran soldier who in wartime only obeyed mission orders from superiors then in civil duty, no one defends his lifted cross. We are naive of what our old man has gotten into with these gubernatorial operations but another warhead of mass destruction is up his sleeve and he will squeeze the red button to launch it.

This techno-crass-gulag persists in an atrocious humdrum, hazardous psychological conditioning and, to a degree, a perverse monopolized method to treat persons. A quick exit is to sign a *Lifetime Voluntary Removal*—thus terminate our stay at this concentration camp alliance—is our best way out of here and wait until eventually *the man's office* sets us free. That is, none of us is quite loose until we set foot outside of prison's front door, it happens frequent, we step out of one old-fashioned revolving door only to enter a bigger sized compound though tighter traverse space and remote camera-control one. It has been widely known that a prison is a mere reflection of its society and it will not step aside from its captive as much—and as fast—as he wants it to; its trace remains forever. Our majority of *detainees* are certain that to contend this shadowy endeavor is loss of precious walkaway time.

Truthfully, we assimilate a pre-morgues' moribund examinations, quartered, and scavenge aloof as we wait for Santa Claus, Rip Van Winkle—or anybody—a Supernova

to happen even in a hidden nameless bare wasteland's den.
Is television one of humankind's greatest assets? It depends.
Half of us are on lookout for this weekend's basketball
finals pre-game show—as no guard is contracted to show
us this on-screen competitive event—between our Los
Diablos Baker's and Rolando's Magic, as a handful of us
will probably be in the visits lounge.

Granted, one truly does not know what we dearly miss
in our growth until we lose it: family, flexibility, friends, our
awesome fish tank or giant plasmas' fully charged remote
control, cheesecake, apple pie, and etcetera. Bookstores
carry popular paperbacks about gazillion ways to die yet
not one chapter in here to entertain us.

Supplementary tourism mags encourage people to visit
any from thousands of never-before-seen places, except
Clearway Correctional Authorities' grounds. We gasp and
fake a lonely back-and-forth sweat-less nowhere-trot in a
jail cell that makes us thoroughly reconstruct every step of
life's sequence up until now, and beyond this. Let us think
about it, to live under familiar peoples' roofs such as our
aunt, sister or granny's, at nearly fifty years of age along
worrisome afterthoughts, what to do without them? One
cannot imagine. What will happen if this prison did not
exist, who will clothe, shelter, and feed us?

Is *the man's office* attempt to tackle and rattle our
appreciative souls, yours, and whosoever's? Why is life so
hard? Is "us in here" our grandmothers or brothers? Are
"we in here" a friend or a loved one? Can a "detainee" be
anyone of you? Did our Supreme Being manufacture various
proto-prisons to house and feed us, e.g.: a.) Best Life, for
a few, or b.) Average Life for some, and c.) Shitty Life for

millions? And why did He place us in this last slot? We do not know. We can only assume—without blame—that His reasons are plenty, such as, our skin color or perfect heights, our blotched teeth or for our obtained dental crowns championship. For our introverted eunuchs and insecure patients as His endless list goes on-and-on. Yet, prison is not a commonplace to "teach a lesson" to someone with inherited imperfect traits. We are not Adam, Judas Iscariot or Barabbas. Point perceived Universal Architect; may we go home now?

Before we pick up another fictitious book a new thought process will come first, that is, to judge it by its cover; second, to skim its middle plot for complicated text and, finish by reading it from "the end" backwards to its genesis. This last resort is only to remain in suspense throughout it since its main characters' cheating and bemeaning boyfriend's death was illogical. However, now on to probe its real murderers' name or gender since it is yet unknown. A chapter-by-chapter hopscotch until tying its romance, cupidity, betrayal and crime altogether and, just like that, satisfactorily certain of its tragic why. Any type of brainstorm to force our minds to knead ideas properly and as a valid reason to distract colossal amounts of spare time.

Our library needs an uplift of more interest-oriented tomes besides its rows of outdated encyclopedias filled with immigration jargon as none of it instructs us on a clear and simple way out of this legislatorial penal maze. A wonderful surprise would be to attain a "How-To Break Free from Concentration Camps; Vol. 19"—not for dummies or idiots but for detainees, would fill in our gap of idleness. Maybe our welcome to a recent reveal of Dave Kooperfeld's "Never

To Be Seen Transfer Act." We are scared, nervous, yet alive along Confucius' optimistic virtues.

Right now, our deepest longing is to be at home and laugh with *anyone* out there and just talk to them with easy dialogues such as, "How are you?", "Do you know what C-C-A means?", then with an agreeableness hear their sincere responses: "Fiyne! But you—see, I'm from Hartford, so it might-ah stand foe Connecticut Clowns Associates—cause it sho-ain't-thee en-double-ey-cee-pee!" Afterwards, someone else replies, "W-e-l-l, I know the first letter stands for Kaylofornia—*hnnn!* The next two might be for Children's Advocacy Group, somewhere along those lines. It's help for pregnant women." To end with *that one* who never cares about his ambitions or surrounds—"Fuck-I-know!" Yay! The C-C-A way.

Despite these continuous incidental holdups, maybe a genuine aim awaits, a deference, or a confidential message for detainees as a biblical passage about reluctant Jonah humbles us. Who knows? One day they must spit us out of this whale's belly so that we may become unprecedented advocates. However, activists for what? *Felons?* How does a voice for *Illegal Immigration* sound? Representatives of the *Needy?* Our resplendent universe—along with Clearway Correctional Authorities, maintain their own directives for creative awe-inspiring wonders.

We sit cross-legged on a stainless steel stool and on a metal bed frame and stare at each other. Its thin gym mattress and neatly wrapped sheets makes our senses lazy as if those objects induce dreams yet gently tug at us and assuredly invite us to relax and forget about tonight—*Ahw-hum!* Exhaust complete.

GALACTIC WHIRRS

Today's breakfast would not have fooled a kindergartener. Our fat-reduced food, although decent, is of a lunchbox size meal designed to alleviate our hunger urges for a while. A small group of *Special Diet* detainees are lucky to, most of our service times, receive their skimpy meals ahead of everyone else and, regardless of our unforeseen occurrences, on schedule. Their high-strung chronological food intake, pharmaceutical doses, biological nutrient flaws, overboard spiritual mantras and immature tantrums make them distinctive. However though, most times our guards are unaffected by any ceremonial entreaties, family rituals, or cultural doctrines as their favorite phrase is, "we only work here." Our guards are also self-absorbed, heartless, and not free; they too fit a gruesome Good Samaritan crime scene.

3:00 P.M. count, our quietest period in our day besides nighttime. If a paperclip lands on our dayrooms' spit-shine cement floor it will echo, as blue whales' shriek songs, gyrating every cell. However, our permeated whir is of an occult ventilator's motor that hums its cold air wall-to-wall, ceiling-to-floor, back-and-forth; it is almost visible every time it gives us goosebumps, makes us shiver and it sounds spooky too. We have not seen any icicles from its grille frame, yet.

Outside, a ticktack chime of our guards' keys as he approaches each door and shouts surnames to hear booking numbers in response. He wears a holster belt that includes a baton, handcuffs, a can of pepper-spray and a two-way radio that flusters incoherent codes that make him discoverable.

Throughout those quiet recesses most of us lay on our beds, eyes closed, and repose. Tower-like Tree-Top is at a family visit. "Our Daily Bread" is our most fully accessible text, and in various versions and languages, as we reflect on its well-known historical passages with its same token mindful that in a bling-bling of a given milli-second any one of us may go bonkers—and no one will turn his other cheek or ask for forgiveness. Furthermore, jailbirds are His Word's most devout, upright and faithful followers—for a limited time! That is, until we are set free. Afterwards, we return to sinful lives continuously breaking society's laws and some bills that are still in our legislator's congress awaiting approval, then, without minding our misdeeds, enclose ourselves in yet another brand new—and perhaps more innovated and sophisticated—prison to praise Jesus' name again. *Shoots*! We might bow, turn both cheeks, and praise anyone in exchange for our exonerations. *Oh-Dear.*

Spatial stillness; count time again. Once our sum of numbered flesh clears with an affirmative from their principal tower's riflemen, and about thirty minutes before dinner, our locked doors should re-open. Meanwhile, we peep—for a tenth time again, through our doors' vertical diminutive windows, everyone hovers at three tattoo-steeped new arrivals as they stand in our dayroom's television area with three white pillowcases full of state issues beside their legs. Los Diablos gangsters, probably. We never know who will enter our front door; always an uneasy breath-taking star awaits us—as it will not be our Dominnoy's Dough delivery dude. At first sight, they seem mature and hefty, baldheaded old-timers barring that in this facility's complacency no one participates in street or prison rivalries, yet. Displaced to a far-off country is more austere than to fight or shank ourselves.

More important, we know of this compounds' misfortunate label of *SGT's*, Security Group Threats. These supposed anarchists, dissidents or expatriates are under strict monitor by undercover investigators for our general populace morale. They are pried upon from behind *closed doors* because to our prison it is monumental that those, separate but equal, prisoners' previous prison performances is perused—before transferred, for any outstanding high-risk crimes, until now, as our guards' safety is presumably affirm, those three newbies will remain with us. Maybe this is our truest reason everyone keeps to himself, at times, that is. Anybody's name that lands on its abhorred black book will not help ones' plea when it reaches any honorary justice's hands to make individual determinations. Insurgents; terrorists; free-mind devils, in fewer words.

In a couple of minutes, we will exit our cells to get ready for dinner, as fast as our barricade's total body count correlates with their command tower's summary. Presently, before our majority receive our meals, about a dozen men get an altered dietetic menu. Some of them concede of their food allergies and diabetes, low-sodium and high-sucrose recipes, meat-lovers and vegans, pontifical sacrifices, exaggerated illnesses and fanatical liturgies. Don't ask, don't tell; we have it.

One of them is "Gyro" from Greece, a self-professed Mediterranean foodie, claims to suffer from *hamburgernitis*, he insists that if he does not eat countryside raised tender lamb meat, *au vin*, medium-rare, every day at sunset his tendinitis disables him thus transforms into a very *enraginitis, avenginitis* guest. He will drop a saucy veggie burger patty on a kitchen's oily and dirty rubber mat, put it back on a fancy plate and serve it, only to save his weekly balance sheet. "Gyro", our culinary chef, is a risky potato famine type of person therefore a threat to society; he too fits a food outbreak criminal scenario. Our main-line food does not fulfill us, their delicate diets is meager compared to ours, and they seem succumb and frail; they are shapeless.

Moreover, from an institutional foodservice manufacturer's standpoint, where is our alimentary crops processed at, and how? That is, some of us are not aware of dangerous food-borne bacteria or digestive poison risks that result from different contact forms of which include inadequate serving temperatures, sanitary hygiene and safety negligence resulting in salmonella, E. coli and Bovine Spongiform Encephalopathy: Cuckoos Cow Cancer, or Mad Cow Disease.

"Continue to remember those in prison as if you were together with them in prison, and those who are mistreated as if you yourselves were suffering." Hebrews 13:3; the Bible.

A new day is underway as we are inside of our units waiting 10:00 A.M. count's clearance. We are devastated, one of prison's setbacks is to not relish our sun's daily early rise or awe its dusk. Within our cells, a copycat eclipse of our moon comes by every night at lights-out and in the morning as a spectacular incandescent. Tree-Top has tangled himself between his bed sheets, half-naked, he sleeps like a kitten. This facility is unlike many corrective centers where at every daytime count *all* imprisoned men must be awake, fully clothed, and sitting upright on every bunk.

After our breakfast, as we all get up and away from our metal tables, some of us clumsily strike an errant crossbar below it and now some of our left kneecaps have lumped aching bruises. Our guideline to follow in here is, no blood—no doctor—no pills, even if with a limp. Our diner-dash-dayroom tables are unsafe; they have an unwieldy underneath steel design and some of us are unhappy when our shins bang its base hinges. Thankfully, no one has fractured a tibia or broken a leg, yet. Those defected tables also fit a defective recall crime scene; maybe we should be more careful next time but we always forgive and forget.

Two weeks ago—and by convicts' presumptiveness, a genesis of deteriorated tooth upsets caused me to fill a *Dentist Docket Request* and marked its main reason as a *check-up only*. It does not matter if we mark its check box *"Emergency if Blood, Non-Emergency if No Blood"*, our slips are stored in secured bins and whenever our dentist's aide has spare time, collects our vouchers. Anyhow, as if to reciprocate for a backwards moonwalk act when inserting my voucher—prickly as she was in a haste to get out of our pod—and for good reason because it is where every danger lies, amongst our condemned.

Besides, our routine dental inquiries such as gingivitis,

tartar, or plaque build-ups contain no valid reasons for our lone and exultant director of dentistry, as he is restricted to handle *real emergencies only*: ruptured lips, bleeds that cascade, knocked-out teeth and dislocated jaws incidents, for example.

His new-hire college-bound anesthetic aide who browsed me with a harmonious back-and-forth tilt of her neck and shoulders, promised to *fix it* at some future consult though not until "it is in a state of acute distress, anomalous inflammation or disconcerted hemorrhage." A straightforward memo, as if to concede that my request docket has one more slender opportunity to reach our top ten list of their enormous agenda as this compound is not a general hospital. *Thanks for your inopportune out-of-space and out-of-bounds visit. See-yah!*

Yippee! I made it. "Welcome," our nurse said as she quickly turned her smile into a stare as if she just saw an alien, and not my alien number that she first verified but an outer space creature. Was it because of my supinely and comfort posture on the dentist's horizontal chair as she inched away from my mouth's checkup? With an outstretched arm—plus a dental mirror's handle length, she saw my gape and asked if I had any strength left to shut it back down? She looked around and immediately grabbed a light-blue handkerchief, covered her nose and stopped short of requesting a spacecraft uniform.   Afterwards, she began to safari inside of what to her it might have been a severely neglected Arizona's Grand Canyon with blight and defective forms of parasites and spoiled microorganisms as they barely survive inside. She came to extinguish everything that moves and smells and to rescue whatever she could.

From an optical telescopic view, my mouth's rear looks like an archeological playground as only a few dentists have profoundly excavated it, and always disguise it with their disgusted looks at that same old creek-smell drainpipe where once a tooth grew, chewed, and died. Now, it is a black void where a microscopic metal brace hides in its black hole thus causes a pulse of discomfort under its soft, boneless gum tissue and sends a throbbing message to my brainy forehead. Also, further inside of my mouth, next to its tonsils, jabs another itty-bitty boney kibbled artifact in deliberate descent. My sensible tongue has invisible bruises from rubs and from a pushy play of tumble with those *things* without success—especially with food scraps camouflaged as molecular defenders inside of those craters.

Albeit, to choose one tooth from among its neighborly disfigured fragments will excruciate me more than its extraction for someone within our dentistry declared that undue use of anesthesia is standard protocol. Let me see if whomever will grind, and pull off, those bones has the capability to knock both nuggets off with a single hack. Denture skeleton number seventeen has a black bothersome blunt, which is in misery and heaven-forbid-need of an odonatologist to yank it; this one surpasses my leftover caverns as their bulls-eye goner.

Toothaches, nerve damage, infected gums and swollen cheeks have a quick fix: an aspirin to shoo us and to dissemble our intrusive visit, and as he recommends to every sufferer, "A nine-hundred gram double-dose of acetaminophens will suffice." As our only and last opportunity to find out whether their jocular Russian roulette games with our dentures, an extraction for post-mortem preserve—display and study, or a simple heavenly fortuity, no one knows.

Did Zeus strike a rod, without consent, and rescued my afflicted cogwheel? Is it their mere pretenses to save our prison ecosystem from airy fungus pestilence, its parametric ozone layer from disintegration, or its climate change to preserve detainees' cancerous lungs? Alas, they will presumably enact its immediate removal along its disturbed piece of nickel that is past oxidization inside of its landfill cavity—and ruining its partners.

Lately, as if that toothache will murder me anytime soon, now compulsively read liturgical passages from deceased dignitaries and extra-terrestrial aliens on a daily basis. In consequence, presence at every church service has become an obsession, and to pray for patience, for peace, and purposeful auspice. On a metaphysical scope, is it my mouth's dire decay or its last crumbled piece of bone inside of its abyss beseeching a split-second plead of innocence? Alternatively, is it a radical phone dial for a superior barricade's dentist second opinion to prolong its imminent disintegrative phase?

On some nights, that speck's non-supportability gives me nightmares about a disconcerted ogre-like grave robber chasing me in-between our dayroom tables with wire-cutting pliers and garden shears as he stabs, jerks, jabs and belittles, "What pain punk?" Root canals are worrisome; they are creepy. Nevertheless, their experimental prognoses considered, *has* that rotten molar *really* asked for forgiveness, and in turn, my responsibility to consult with a tooth fairy to suppress its metamorphosis? *Hah.*

Today's Christian Science seminar inspired everyone.

We surmised that in truth we have a meaningful purpose in our treks for our permanence inside of this barricade: That is, to share His divine word and love amongst ourselves—though Jesus knows we can do it outside too. Our fellowship who visit us said that no matter what type of perturbed monotony we are involved in, we are still *H-i-s* precious creation—therefore, we are valued *more* outside of this place!

An elemental companionship zeal that reinforced our collective need for a holy heal so that we may access true happiness in our wicked lives, more so if becoming constructive persons is within our plans. Spirituality is being *one* with our Lord, Humanity, and in communion with this elegant universe that surround us—indeed—we can be more than one-thousand percent whole and happier in our free earthly expanse.

Most influential, for a queer reason I am feeling an inward magnificent appreciative serenity and mindfulness, a nirvana. Is it one of those post-hallucinate side effects from my smoked big fat joints? A factor of this inner calm is that we must not be in here to start uproars, shake-the-spot, or hurt anyone; those youthful reckless years are in our Black Hole's depth. In coincidence to turn our unruly missions around, our Christian service volunteers taught us how to remove toxic thoughts from our minds as it may be beneficial in our road to psyche and physical wellness; "healthy mind equals healthy body," they said. A new way forward to relinquish anger, animosities, inner conflicts, unremorseful propensities and subsequently, to overturn those ill and energy drainers and fervors with positivism, optimism, and goal-oriented perseverance.

Conclusively, our germination of this opulent humble

imploration, self-forgiveness and to forgive those who have wronged us is imperative. It means to continue practicing gratefulness, forthright, and remaining open-minded to any superior educative material presented in our spirit-energized ceremonies by adherence, introspect, and to absorb benefits out of their sincere reconstructive feedbacks. At times, those theological doctrines make me feel meaningless, infinitesimal, and unworthy of existence. Nonetheless, to belong is fun, essential and hearty, good night my adored unbounded flock of multicolored starry galaxies.

———

"Count time! Count time! Count time!" Shouted aimlessly into our dayroom our lead guard thus everyone wriggled into their cells.

A minute later, a back-up guard screamed, "We're missing one!"

"He's in the showers!" Hollered our first guard.

The second guard walked a few steps to our shower stalls and childish boasted, "Why are you in there during count time?"

Naked, surprised, and with shampoo bubbles over my entire body, blindly yelled back, "What time is it sir?"

Increasing a hasty raucous tone, he bellowed, "Get out and go to your cell right now—go!—go!—go!"

Lagging—as if approaching a guillotine's ebb—dragged my wet nakedness into our cell to finish birdbathing, dried, and dressed. Afterwards, relieved and refreshed, picked up a deformed sci-fi softcover, laid on my bed, and waited for our trivial process to unfold. Tranquil.

Tree-Top is at our library in research of immigration

law; he says he does it only to *kill* idle jitters. An undisputed majesty, with his muscular body, herculean strength, and rationale of a brute, he may legally bare-hand assassinate a grizzly in a no-hunting zone, and not receive a blemish. He may sell its fur, jawbone and collectible toes on the black internet market; he too fits a cyberspace crime scene. *Seesaw* is his groove and, my suspicion is that he senses my ridiculous and hypocrite flatter. *Humph!* Any trick to survive; a fair handshake from him has become my homework and to not disrupt *his* space, my strategy.

Nevertheless, he is copy-i-n-g our old man's techniques at how-to decipher municipal, state and federal legal codes. Great, those law encyclopedias are a purposeful commodity to confuse us even more, and, most are outdated like our *premier* television episodes. Where is Angus MacGyver or Owe Jay's Dream Team to come to our aid?

Our men who placed store purchases last week received it today.

Most of us stock up on coffee and sweetbreads as some of us must have caffeine to remain awake and vigilant throughout our day, and nighttime too.

Whereas some men endure irregular sleep patterns through episodes of sluggishness, melancholy, and hopelessness, others make a living out of this place even if some of their cases' rigid complexities such as drug traffic, human smuggling or repeat border-crossing offenses and its dumbfound thought of a possible return to their far-off countries of origin overwhelms them. A morbid consequence to have to leave their wives and children behind, some of their kids even forgotten and, in most helpless heartbreak scenarios, without income and love and educational support.

Our "American Dream", over. Men that erect murals do not unite families; they separate them.

Anyway, Tree-Top did not purchase many goodies for our lack of money. Nevertheless, we maintain everyday hygienic toiletry. Besides, we have a munchies vending machine in an adjacent anteroom although we access it with our guards' escort only. It operates with a prepaid debit card; cash is abstract and prohibited by our barricade's statutes but cryptically available for obscure transactions.

Upon sunrise, one detainee went home and handed Tree-Top a pair of headphones for us to listen to music on our cells' built-in radio antenna. He also left behind a couple of intact text materials for us to keep busy throughout our lethargic body enumerations, which are thrice per day as they begin at 10:00 A.M., 3:00 and 8:00 P.M. Although it may do done whenever they *feel* that one of us escaped, and continue our count twice more during graveyard shift while we sleep. Out in our free markets, ranchers also perform similar jobs except that they tally chickens, pigs, horses and prairie animals. *Mooooh!*

Friday: laundry exchange. Simple. We handout one sock and receive one in return. We handout two; receive one, with luck. We handout four socks and receive two, excessive clothes is against compound rules. This interactivity fulfills in our dayroom's empty middle and overlooked by a guard. As he emptied a wheeled hamper of clean garments on its floor, we tried to form a straight line though noticed that our exchange is on a first-come first-serve basis, so we disintegrated—and just like that, our gig ended. Some of us prevent this needless chaotic surge as we hand-wash our uniforms in our sinks or while we shower and, especially, our undies because in this way we are sure of its soapy cleanliness, chlorine scent, microbe safe and heartfelt snuggly sporty.

In theory, our dirty laundry process is through its complete immersion in sanitary fluids, rinsed, and dried at extreme temperatures to corrode germs, fungi and microorganisms yet, nonetheless, my white boxer-short has an eye-opener, a caramel or toffee ugly skid marks on its front and rear. A miniature t-shirt is too tight and has yellow sweat stains around its underarms; whereas my orange jumpsuit is monstrous so its return is necessary since my orange costume is of an unfit firefighter. Without complaints, simply asked our guard for a decent swap and he joked, "Your size will come from *Macy's* next week on a fire engine." So much needless commotion for our *Black Friday* frenzy as our best *fitting room* stage is to gauge and exchange our uniforms among ourselves inside of our cells.

After every count, our no-carbs, no-protein, no-dairy delegates is first to eat, without a doubt, our gourmet connoisseurs. Some of them behave somewhat jumpy, as if greedy Armenian detainees might snatch their delicacies as the rest of us linger inside of our locked units and anxiously peep every few seconds as we wait for their fine diner's experience to finish. Also, those of us accustomed to give grace before our meal times abstain because by the time our prayer is finished, a fruit or a biscuit goes adrift. Afterward, our guard loosens our herd of carnivorous folks—but only to hold us again for our deep-fry food's arrival, which is usually gelatinized.

Pod "Z" has a capacity for seventy detainees though right now we are about sixty; we have not had a full house, so far. Our guards announce church worship services and, perfunctorily, six of us attend those distinguished sermons, which take place in our rec room only a few feet perpendicular to our pod. Normally, we encourage ourselves to make every joy-filled convents to hear enthusiastic and to stimulate new ideas from appreciative preachers and a potpourri of pilgrims and hard-core ex-cons—these last group of men have repented from always being a perfect fit to any crime scene. An underlined otherworldly ploy is that Tree-Top *needs* to calmly seek Confucius, Genghis Khan, his Platonic love or just to encounter his right counselor before he seriously hurts someone. That is, to expunge his mind from *Seasaw Solitary State Ward* would be wonderful.

Although playing hand cards keeps me away from Tree-Top, nevertheless, this nasty flow of exiting to meet with our contemporaries only to play double-six dominoes, checkers and, curiously and admittedly, Monopoly's "Go To Jail" pitfall bewilders as one cannot ignore and skip that dammed square. Herein, we land on that troubled square, hence, we had better adapt to games that include honest and decent children's board frolics such as SCRABBLE, JUMBULAYA and UNO. Regardless, when we ignore our televised ads it alleviates us—as it may give us a dispirited or bluey mood to see children, teenagers and adults have fun in fabulous regale parks—some of which we have visited.

Lastly, an inability to watch what we wish to watch whenever we wish to watch and from wherever we wish to watch saddens us as we are in watchful grounds twenty-four hours per day. Cool as ice, our board jollies aid us and keeps our minds afloat and away from our veiled jailhouse's tense troublemakers as well as we hold our repressed and incarcerated anger meter low and gleeful inspirits high.

Our cell doors g-e-n-t-l-y opened for us to step outside in unison to our dayroom and hang around for dinner at five p.m., afterwards a church service at six p.m., supposedly. That is, many times an announcer for a certain clerical ceremony arrives followed by our guards canceling it for unknown reasons. Evil forces patrol overtime our space command center.

For our past two weeks, an attempt to figure our satellites' programs is futile; it airs inconsistent shows that our guards control. As we learn to maneuver a myriad of inefficient, lopsided inventive patterns to pick up a routine and make our time fly in an easy, calm, laid-back manner and— *whammoe!* We are stuck in *the hole.*

This is our third day of total lockdown so we must perform every customary biological necessity locked inside of our cells, for example, eat, defecate, launder, birdbath, and play various tabulations of solitaire. We gamble our candies and potato chips on chess or poker matches with our cellie as this also takes care of mammoth down time, if he knows how to play any type of cards such as Rummy, Blackjack or Texas Hold'em as most men are not American-raised. If not, we have plenty of time to teach someone new tricks—afterwards, to win his goodies is our goal.

Our routine activities are in shutdown mode because of an inconspicuous intrusion of an unknown disease-infused paras-*ite* into our pod—and *ite* is not us; *ite* hates us. So far, its red key pandemonium descriptive term is "apparent", for in any jail no inmate ever knows any sensitive top-secret matters. One of ours, who just disengaged from *Mental Observatory Bureau* a couple of days ago, said that he *saw* five sick patients *inadvertently* fetched in here even before toxicology reports revealed their exam residuals to this transferrable illness. *Sheesh.* These guys were brought in here from the *MOB* unit, its shorter name. Now, whether too late or not, for sciences' sake, they are in a full-pledge consternation and unsure if their outbreak is malaria, anthrax, or mumps. We recite for those in-patients' rescue before we die.

None of us is certain of any specifics of these sick men, such as their physical well-being, medical health or state of thought, whether they walked into our pod on their own feet or if hauled in here by our guards. So, we assume that our medical personnel sent our warden an urgent e-mail to insert everyone in an unspecified quarantine, or until their examinations become clear. Luckily, we will never know their conclusions; be it their suspicions, and ours.

Oscar Meyers—not the hot-dog man but our real Peruvian friend, filed a complaint to their second-in-command to explain his previous experiences and insights concerning this facility's incompetent staff as they handle this pathological pandemonium and more—maybe even deadly—plagues. Indeed, we need to express those faults in paper form and slide them through their proper channels even *if* those papers may end up shredded—as they are untraceable—in some dumpster and appeased by our feeble guards when they talk to their superiors about sarcastic mysteries: "What papers? Who has a flu? We have a sickness in here? AH1N1—what! Is this somebody's penitentiary number?" That is their lazy norm, foggy posture and standard procedure.

Their hushed circled avoidance raises doubts, why are guards, general staff, and nurses with protective facemasks and latex gloves when they expedite and overturn our pod and, why *we* do not have access to one to lower our risk. Are *we* not mortals? As is, our barricade's brand is *detainees* as a formal charge is not in process before any law decision-maker, prosecutor or defense attorney, and we are not federal convicts, yet. We are held in a tank with an indefinite timespan and without our most basic due process of law: legal defense. Up until now, we are in an unjustified gulag exactly as Middle Easterners inside of Cuba's Guantamo Bay. Darn close but no cigars in here.

Notwithstanding, we are grateful for our daily provisions yet we notice our lack of proteins, a misery of vitamins, inorganic calcium and supplemental carbohydrates and vital nutritious minerals necessary for robust physique hoopla. Without fail, domestic and foreign-grown maize is probably one of many cheap grains on agricultural markets today— and our daily bread: tortillas, grits, biscuits, muffins, puddings and flakes. It is okay, we Hispanics thrive on corn. Clearway Correctional Authorities is, well, our Corn Crib Alliance, or last line of subsistence provider.

Tree-Top snoozes an entire day; to slumber during sunshine is not me. In a daydream and within my rational timeframe when inserted in this barricade, a ray of hope lifted me about a hasty exit but it voyaged into a galactic black hole. Until now, it has been eighteen days, and counting, since they registered us in here and although surreptitious and inopportune, nonetheless, whomever has a vis-à-vis date with destiny?—And, had we known about this abduction, to postpone it would have been better as some survivalist's affairs may be controlled—to an extent, while manmade phenomena incomprehensible. Life is life.

Regardless, it has been over a week since we purchased foodstuffs and mine belatedly arrived with its ballpoint and postal utilities, body lotions, and a few dehydrated soups. Comparatively, those essentialities are not as paramount as an irresistible—handle-with-care—fragrant and insatiable *Snicker's* chocolate bar. *Mmmm!* To save it until my way home was an illogical good idea, mindful that by who-knows-when, it might spoil and a waste of a sinful crunchy dessert. Above our dedicated worship of its sweetness and scrumptiousness thereof is an irresistible and god-mandated yearning and drooling for *one* while those nearby savor theirs.

Equally handy, a prepaid phone card is included in my brown paper bag—which we have to purchase at ten cents each—and prices are going up. It may be that these items to communicate will be handy as our uncertain transfer to *any* of Immigration and Child Endowment's thousand hold sites across the United States and our magical sum of jail time assimilates to Advanced Algebra: an unknown factor.

Clearway Correctional Authorities' lock-up is a variety of calculus analogous to Einstein's famous scientific formula $E=MC^2$. Our logical, perhaps misunderstood Algebraic exponential is, whereas, (C) (S) (T) = I^2? In plain words, Crime multiplied by Sentence multiplied by Time equals Incarceration Squared Questionable. Our ancient Greek demigod and mathematician Pythagoras would be in here, caved as a *detainee of interest*, unfazed and tugging his last three strands of hair, twirling his tummy-ebbed grey beard vainly attempting to resolve this incongruent theorem.

Immigration and Child Endowment, Task of Home-Field Security, Borders and Bridges Protectors have labeled us *detainees* in absence of a crime, informal sacrifice of sentences, our length of time we will be *under investigative review,* and exactly how long is *"we don't know."* That is our guards' main answer to our "right-to-know" inquiries. Even so, we serve jail time without a federal indictment or conviction or a court date on their overbooked calendars—which are longer than a Red Shrimp's logbook on a Mother's Day evening.

Whoosh! We are still in lockdown status, or quarantine, or solitary housing, or caged until a new decree develops from our hospital's personnel, a foreign Centralization of Diseases Command or a domestic Federal Drug and Cure Allies or our World Wellness Watch. These agencies may say today—tomorrow, next week or month, ten thousand years from now or until someone finds a cure to Parkinson's disease, cancer and AIDS.

Right now, birdbaths are in demand, that is, splish-splashing soapy sink water over our bodies like wild drakes, at least, for those of us who are accustomed to shower daily. Our dirty water overflows onto the dayroom and our idle guards, on their paydays, will mop it though most often our *pod messenger* that runs errands outside takes care of it. One time he did a backdoor speedy mailer, slipped on a puddle and almost cracked his shaved shiny skull.

Our cell is located about fifteen feet from one of our

two digital displays and it keeps us distracted as we watch various sports presentations from our cells vertical windows. For instance, in South Africa's Confederates Cup semi-finals tournament, the United States men's soccer team encountered a heavily favored Spain team but won two to nil. A great delight that took care of two long hours of inactivity; props to our U.S national team for their show-off victory to Sunday's trophy centerpiece.

Our mealtime grand-finale show diverted us from our overly defrosted dry chunk of Midwest Mamma's Meatloaf, semi-raw Macedoine carrots and a grainy mush of Mediterranean couscous, which we are thankful. Besides, we eat every grain of food because it is obligatory—as our mini-portions do not replete our tummies. We are on a low-fat and low-calorie, low-sugar and low-sodium and low-ingredients strict nourish plan. *Slim-Jim Shakes? Huh.*

Despite their apologetic watchful measures of our food pyramid and body mass index, every day dull exercises and disjointed yoga clones yet somehow these accounts makes us feel mindful yet modest, hungrier yet satisfied, and merry which beats melancholia. Even to remain isolated is hard to attain within this errant compound. My strict physical routine is fifty-fifty: push-ups and sit-ups, that is. Moreover, we act out effortless ta'i-chi moves, taekwondo kicks and muscle stretches while we visualize a slice of chocolate cake topped with *crème fraîche* and a sparkled stemmed cherry on top eases our jitters.

Whenever we do not perform constructive activities, we lye on our beds an entire day and hallucinate about what it might be like to live on planet Mars. In contrast, this experience is like a storied man who is lost in a desert craving water and—as he weakens, sees an elusive oasis. Family is family.

Finally, before end-of-day lights-out, Tree-Top birdbaths. Meanwhile, my midway read of Patterson's' teeth-clenching fast-pace novel, "The Big Bad Wolf", withholds my sleep. This before-bed book is bold and brain-building bravery—*ahuuuhhhh!*

THEIR BIG BAD *IF*

Our great news: As a hazy morning unfolds, rumors that our preventive crisis, deadlock, will clear today pumped us up. *Awesome!* Our guards gossiped that our warden will address every issue that has arisen and our concerns of their unexpected shutdown of our habitual pastimes. Every board game will return to the dayroom and our methodic undertakings will restart, we wait.

At once, our cell doors hesitated sideways, gap after gap a few inches at a time and, forcibly and inexplicably, twitched and opened and everyone careened outside like hyenas in horror shrill and shouts, "Yes! Yahoo! Yay-yow!" Most men rushed to grab our two isolated handsets; the rest of us formed a line to wait for one to become available. Forasmuch as these involuntary emergencies happen sporadically, afterwards every phone freak demands a fifteen-minute talk-time limit, as our majority are desperate to let someone outside know that we are fine from a swine.

We exited our cells, legs and arms extended, with an immediate need to body-flex, do aerobics, and to walk more than three steps in our attempt to knock down our nerves around our dayroom—for this *is* our most urgent need. Our DNA's beauty is not to procrastinate or remain frozen, as our natural proof is that even when we sleep, we move. Our cells' breadth is too narrow to move freely and for complex energy-consummation and re-energized physical exercises.

Again, within a short time, we inclined at our pre-arranged board stratagems of chess, spades, dominoes, and to converse about invented hobbies that kept us busy those three days of tiresome immobility besides our three steps to reach our cell's toilet and four to its door. Mostly everyone did similar activities: slept, read, meditated, exercised and bathed, bird style.

Quickly, our Kaiser entered our unit with two uniformed escorts—staunch and adamant—headed to our dayroom's center, which is as somber as Mars, we slowly and attentively huddled in front of their compressed posture, like pups to learn new tricks from their master in exchange for a kibbled treat. We surmised these three ravens were not in here to abide in peace, but to give us trouble. Our chief custodian is a middle age blonde white man with a medium physique, crystal blue eyes, dressed as an executive banker, and at first view represents a fair, God-fearing family fellow.

Immediately, all three men surveyed up and around our pod then our warden cleared his throat, and began his anticipated speech with a direct and loud belligerent rhetorical remark:

"Is anyone in here not understand what your term *detainee* means?" His fingers snapped and gestured toward a mass of Hispanics, switched his view their way, and in sardonic tone said, "Oh, I'm sorry. I forgot about your Spanish speakers." We hoped he would not forget to set us free.

Amidst our crowd of men from different origins emerged

a young Mexican, who had just arrived from *Deehachapi's Penitentiary* maximum security, to translate our gatekeeper's long-awaited message. As a scammer know-how and willful reversal of words, spoke our warden's first sentence, "Quien se quiere ir a la casa?" (Who wants to go home?) Mostly everyone, our majority Mexicans, started to wail in riot crescendo—"Yo! Yo! Yo!" (Me! Me! Me!)

Now our mischievous youngster gave us a reason for his whacked message delivery, feistily added, "Esto es injusto porque nos tienen sin fianza, sin avogados del estado, sin cargos, y ahora con una enfermedad mortal." (This is unjust because they have us in here without bail, without state attorneys, without charges, and now with a deadly disease.)

The warden interrupted and raised both arms in contempt, increased his imposed tone, "Hold-hold-hold! Will someone explain to me what he just said?"

Our translator moderately answered, "Yes, we want to go home because we could die in here from this freaking disease and no one will ever know about it."

"Oh yes! Your swine flu. W-e-l-l-h, I have compromised with our medical experts about it and they have given me a green light to restart your program today. Safely."

Though, as he speaks about our ghostly practical team of nurses—for they are not present to corroborate on this panicky infectious pandemic, somehow connived his speech into an opportunity to detail his barricade's monetary costs incurred to protect and maintain our welfare.

He took a deep breath to regain his composure while he computed numbers, aghast, added, "You guys wanna-know, it costs five-hundred dollars per each of you guys—only to *see* a doctor." As he created indexing gestures, half-heartedly sneered, "These can dramatically rise with analysis, preventive measures, discovery, hospitalization, treatment, medicaments, and aftercare *if* one of you is infected with this AH1N1 virus." To end, slouched his head and sadly said, "And this breaks my heart."

After all, this barricade has its independent fishy infirmary; therefore, no need to incur transport costs. Additionally, whenever we encounter absurd scenarios, transfer of a detainee that needs crucial care to a local hospital, or to dummy-ride, our barricade's breadbaskets *is* their preferred method since its enclosures are beyond *Brink's Banking Safeguard.* A meat wagon will not ride anyone free of charge.

Besides, *what if?* No one is sick. *What if?* Our men only had a common chill. *What if?* We put these men in Seesaw's special cubicles. *What if? What if? What if?*

True, bacterial preventive steps is a wise and proper alternative. Mystically, he never brought it up as he sustained, "Your three men suspected to have flu-like symptoms will be housed in a different dormitory *only if* their exams return positive." Again, our pathologists are not present to confirm or deny this urgent matter, their plan thereof—or at least to educate us about this illness so that we may have peace of mind. Our warden *may* say that we live in Xanadu then return to his executive furnished and cellular-controlled comfy chamber, *the man's office,* in devilish laughter murmur, "Ha! They believed me and now they are under a team of nurses' care."

Three days after our awareness of this malicious curse, our chief immediately began to absolve himself from a repercussive report or a class-action lawsuit as he shifted responsibility to our barricade's medicinal diplomats—an absent first-aid team of nurses, matter-of-factly accused, "They're the ones that call some heavy-duty shots in these instances."

Amongst us, we also have *Foreigners* who know beans about our English language; they are under a false alert that we will head home. These men belong to many far-off countries such as China, Armenia, Pakistan, Czechoslovakia, Libya, and from around planet earth. For that reason, in sign language, we began to make an all-across-our-board bulletin that no one will get out anytime soon. Word of our warden.

Unanticipated, one *detainee's* input: "Let us transform one of our many pods for men that show specific signs of crippled sicknesses, are curved into humanity's smoky flue of no return, or dying."

"Unfeasible!"—exclaimed our warden. This lucrative barricade is no cemetery; we have no room for more unclaimed cadavers.

Alternately, a second inmate's idea: "Stop our flow of new parolees from partnered barricades whom are marked with positive or incurable diseases, those that indiscreetly arrive every day."

"Impossible!"—he rejected. Insinuating that prisons make money by its occupancy of beds, not to store empty ones holding air like balloons.

Ultimately, a third convict's concept: "Release everyone without a criminal charge."

"Preposterous!" He retorted. Once more, our barricade's budget is beyond debate. Decode: bonuses, prizes, incentives and allotments.

Unknown sources, *detainees,* guess that fiscal statistics at Clearway Correctional Authorities charges Washington about $420.00 daily per individual. Here is a closer estimate: we are over 1,100, which equals somewhere around $462,000.00 daily and $168,630,000.00 yearly, in this barricade alone. Dozens of more migrant hold centers exist located mostly in uninhabited coast-to-coast areas within the United States.

Noticeably, human *detention*, like citizen's arrest, is an enterprise such as Bail Bonds businesses and in practice, anyone with lots of money or one who owns or rents residences may transform those into hold facilities—with its required legal paperwork to perform business, of course. It is free to go to jail but it may cost a fortune to get out of a hole. Small inner-city hotels and roadside motels will transform into *intermediary centers* as they reasonably acknowledge its ancillary monetary profits preferably to run a cheap routine lodge saloon. Soon, those inns will inevitably leave their neon logos flashing "No Vacancy", permanently. Men at work, *on prisons,* ahead. Build it, and they will come

Tomorrows' presupposed court date, a medley of concerns makes one uneasy. That is, with our alarmed incessant flu virus some of our court proceedings are in suspense. Our most abhorred intermissions are, first, whenever no one sees any televised programs as this means that our "now showing" is a rerun and, second, whenever everyone is standing by his cell it means that someone will get tossed, and third, whenever our dayroom is in extreme quietness it means that someone went home. Accordingly, a quick jump into our showers is best to become fully awake and start to re-apprehend cleanliness, upbeat moods, and renewed character. Meanwhile, in a 2009 Confederates' Cup soccer semifinal, its host South Africa will play against a star-studded Brazilian team and this will be fun to watch, as it is underway.

We had dinner: a lumpy mass of noodles with a hint of meat, maybe bits of ground beef, about two ounces of cabbage, an overloaded tablespoon of sweet corn, a crumbly thin slice of rice cake, and five ounces of colorless insipid punch; we are grateful for our well-balance diet. For this reason, our inquiry into a possibility of a bi-weekly purchase of merchandise to stock up always goes unheard through our guards' ears. Thankfully, *if* hunger strikes us again, we have delicacies such as *Top Ramens*, *Fishtank Tuna* and *Oyster Jerky* to fill any gaps in our stomachs and once those party favorites are gone, that is all for our week's remainder, and it might rollover two consecutive weeks.

Brazil eliminated South Africa from its home spectacle, 1-0. So now, they must play a buoyant United States team again in an attractive final as their first rendezvous ended 3-0: advantage Brazil.

Our sorry despicable news: my court date is hours away, however, with some of our feverish ailments, our motions are set for reschedule. For instance, one *detainee* had his audition set until June of next year—and it's only October! Another one had *his* forwarded until April yet our majority are due in court in six months, more or less. What will happen to each of us? *Humm.* We do not appreciate this uncertainty—and it is legal, or so they say. This excessive worry about our ordeal's difficult technicalities has me with a possibility to dig a narco-tunnel, or to send an e-mail to our G50 Conglomerate or to fax a photocopy of my passport to our Federal Beerhouse of Immigrants so that they may stamp a visa for a forthwith flight home.

Our self-imploration is in stoppage time against our God-given liberty. However, as a biblical phrase insinuates, here on earth we have a time for everything, and a time for nothing: a time to free it, and a time to embrace it; a time for soul-search and a time for exit-search. A time to listen to System of a Down's "Prison Song" and a time to hum Amazing Grace. A time to say "hi" to our locksmith and a time to say "bye" to him; a time to sit detained and a time to walk out of detainment. A time to be unique and a time to share ourselves. *Amen.*

If our AWOL warden would only march in here alongside a British cavalry and, with his fictitious sympathetic London accent, ask before our still-conscious burial at their backyard phantomlike cemetery, "Pardon, would you prefer some daub on your incognito tombstone? *Petit Papillon*, don't you think? *Almightee Alcatraz*, maybe. Aha! *Shake-spea-y Wuz Hea-y?*"

Just as fast as he entered, announced his good-bye, "Now, if you will excuse me but I must certainly return to my responsibility."

On an opposite angle of our five murals, we are certain that, *i-fh* we reincarnated as free-range cows; we may certainly possess plenty of acreage to roam and fresh-air to breath independence.

FLIGHT MODE

A neighborly marriage of old folks have been visiting for four consecutive weekends and now he looks worried, alarmed, in disbelief and every time he attempts to speak, his breath deflates in an asthmatic rhythm. He is weary when we converse and lacks energy and optimism. His hunched posture toils and his demeanor sadder than mine is. His 75-year-old wife made this two-hour trip with him, however, remains outside of the facility because our visit-room guard did not let her in; he told them that her sleeveless blouse is too provocative therefore prohibited by compound bureaucracy.

Anyhow, within our fluctuated allotted visit time, we construed a plan to oust our young private immigration attorney for his lack of experience during proceedings—and, hence, he is demanding five thousand dollars more! Gross misrepresentation and economical supply-and-demand inflation; he too fits a sort of Ponzi scheme crime scene. Point of fact, our virtual judge and he twaddle about our arid weather and in less than five minutes, their discourse ends with yet another six-month court date and another sack of cash.

At our homestead, they said, that our family is fine

with their quotidian chores: attending their nine-to-fives and return home. Everyone sent warm hellos and energized wishes for a triumphant exit—or at least a bail opportunity to *try* this case as a free man. Our talk was also about this weekend's soccer finale between Brazil and the United States, an exclusive event that they too plan to keep entertained in their days of relaxation. Though it seems strange, every neighbor, gardener, butcher or cashier outside that knows about this precedent said that they miss our big homie that used to make them laugh. Same here.

Sunday's noon attractive showpiece is a positive outlook for our overall wellness, as we must remain busy, especially as some of us are sick, weak, distraught, and depressed. An unrecognized vibe of being drained, sleepy, plus an inner void and lack of motives to do worthwhile tasks breaks us apart. A malaise instinct. By the way, soon, a seminar on self-improvement on Anger Management presented by local support of volunteers to ease our reintegration into society. S-o-h, we need to attend this workshop to allow ourselves relief in different ways though specifically energy to overcome this debilitated post. Help arrives at just an appropriate timeframe and it feels wonderful as a sensation of surprise uplifts ones' spirits when people from outside stops by to gift us a non-robotic smile and say "hello".

In fact, our time has arrived to rectify repressed anger, hidden bitterness, mettle control, and to dissolve those character defects with a process that our evangelists labeled "self-healing" to comprehensively mend ourselves and appreciate those sensibilities more efficiently in future flare-ups. For instance, to humble our alter ego is beneficial as providence knocks on our hearts, and we reject it. Although as we read our Bibles every day is helpful, our sense of any changes that compel in our attitude toward love, peace, charity and harmony bemuses us. Our preachers say that placidity is slow and unnoticed; likewise our liberty from this shoebox.

Occasionally, we are to write petitions, poems, or essays for ourselves to reference and take home:

Even though breaking up is hard to do, we must do it, at once. This symbolic farewell is not so much about our experiments of many different drugs as it is more about our future, our sanity and our families. We are moving forward, drug-free. It is difficult breaking our age-old disastrous habits as our fear of falling short is forever present. This long and eventful bond was like many relationships: introduction, good and bad times, struggles, and a rollercoaster of a ride venturing a safe-haven of sorts for hiding our real emotions and with uncanny destinations that we know of: jails, hospitals, and cemeteries. Indeed, we leave this chaos behind, turning around and taking nothing with us, pursuing new roads is our choice. Becoming addicted to drugs was a mistake and now we are in debt to our *main man in His office.* Having lost this crusade of overcoming it on our own because it is tougher doing it than saying it. We can live happy with this lesson in defeat. Good-bye alcohol and drugs, this way of living is not promising. Here we are sitting nostalgic on our bunks at C-C-A,—though we are sure that beautiful days await. From this juncture forward, we are free men. May our overlooking saints never allow us to relapse into this squalid frame again—as it will for surely reappear and tragedy will be dangerously expecting us. Finally, a 1970's oldie-but-goodie break-up title by The Manhattan's, *"Kiss and Say Goodbye,"* amen.

Unsurprised final score: Brazil 3, United States 2, even as referees annulled a perfect goal netted by Brazil. In plain view, this attractive soccer match gave us plenty of fun as it ended in agony when America's team was up 2-0 at half time. Our majority remained glued to our monitors as our intense hooliganism of its competitors' excellence as we equally cheered both teams. Great for Brazilian fans, as people say, never underestimate a champion's heart. Brazil's victory goals came by their defender Lucio and a pair by forward Fabiano, and for North America's lost cause, midfielder Dempsey and forward Donovan.

Besides their black-and-white movies and shows for most of our day, and to spend long hours in our leisure room with too many board gameplay mortifies us, whereas, we better focus on a new course to inculcate, an expertise or ideals or lore by a brainstorm of our assorted individuals in here. Even though educative matter is enviously limited in this place, save, a miniature version of *Gideon's International* in every cell, we utter its Gospels and Ten Beatitudes heartily. At our twenty-four hour sentences' end, literature is our minds liberty.

"If you constantly have difficulties,
thank heaven for the good training"—
Master Chen Yen (1937-?)[ii]

A NEW WAY FORWARD

"Free at last, free at last."—*Rev. Martin Luther King Jr. (1929-1968)*

2:00 A.M., Clearway Correctional Authorities. Amidst our sleep's fifth exquisite dream layer, every cell door opened. Then a few hard knocks on its doorframe awakened us and semi-conscious twisted my head to see who it might be, thus exhaled upon seeing that it was not Yahveh's Observers or Joe Smitty and Moeroeni but two enormous and brilliant transport bodyguards holding clip boards. A loud hefty voice announced first and last names as three more guards abruptly awakened everyone who was not up yet. They came inside like grave robbers, we were incredulous of Immigration and Child Endowment's clandestine agents verbally forcing us to sign five-page fine print writs, transforming us from prison carrot-suits to casual clothes and quickly shackled and transported us to San Fuego's International Airport.

Once on its runway, we loaded onto an unmarked white jumbo jet, destined to land at various countries in Central America to drop-off nearly one-hundred deportees that had concurred from a bunch of *Hold* facilities in neighboring states. This maneuver's fuzzy completeness lasted about thirty minutes and up into our dark sky we flew.

2:00 P.M. San Pedro Sula, Honduras. A group of about twenty deportees descended our airplane's ramp as a fresh gush of tropical air capsuled my senses and a natural way to inhale ignited within me, a rebirth gasp. As we bypassed a couple of Honduran customs officers that informed us that our country is under a *state of siege* and, thenceforth, we must sprint to our homes. Then, when we walked outside our National Military and Police Force made their existences felt as they circulated shopping malls, banks, private properties and our highway tolls. Besides our security's calibration, it was possible that high-rank politicians were authorized special concessions to move about freely and convene.

It turns out that our republics' governors had set a countrywide *stay* to be enforced within the hours of 4:00 P.M. until 7:00 A.M. *Shucks,* it is aligned with my priority to arrive home which I had not seen in twenty years.

Fortunately, twenty dollars are secure in my socks— prisoner tactics, so a taxi driver charged me ten dollars, handed me a refund, and taxied me home.

By the way, before exiled, some old folks had prearranged a date with a known family that wanted to introduce themselves upon arrival.

On my next gorgeous unbothered sunrise, instinctively and accustomed to a 5:00 A.M. battle buzzer at Clearway Correctional Authorities' clock, got ready, and enjoyed an organic savory cup of coffee and peeked outside, our streets were like a ghost town. At 7:00 A.M., right after breakfast, peeped through our windows again, a lone taxi crawled so quickly ran outside to signal its driver to pull over. He stopped but did not open its doors or let me inside. He said that our nationwide *stay* is to clear at 9:00 A.M., upon his explanation of this political chaos, every hushed aspects since my arrival clicked, though he added that their stand is absolutely no public or private transport vehicles circulating before 9:00 A.M. and after 4:00 P.M. and that he is headed to his home.

Concurrently, my next idea is to walk to this family's house, but he also warned, "Be careful that *they* don't catch you 'cause *they* will take you to jail."

To reach their place on foot is one-hour—though people trespass an agricultural terrain about a hundred acres square known as *las cañeras*, the sugarcane fields. It is illegal for unauthorized pedestrians to cut corners and infiltrate it and if its patrol officers catch anybody in there, they will request a police unit to seize that person. To enter this windy sway of prairie-like bamboo canes, one must descend a loose-soil trench, then ascend a dirt embankment, take a curved thorny pathway to an extended lonely rutted road that leads to a main rotund asphalt that directs streets in four pathways. This walk is two hours if one goes around it.

Additionally, during daylight hours, empty and fully packed eighteen-wheelers swoop by and leave tailed clouds smelling of petroleum mixed with dust that envelope any pedestrians' faces in-so-much-that dirt does have an acrid taste. And with our sun's extreme heat, every smoky overshadow sticks onto our sweaty bodies' clean clothes.

Amidst this sugar plantation are two lowly and smelly swampy puddles, and every day dirty skinny children aged from five to eight years gather and attempt to catch toads and baitfish. These runnels have thrash in and around them;

various insects are visible inside of its rainwater pool and fly over it yet a few transients that come here say its fish is good to eat. I do not think so. These kids' bellies are inflated and warped and their umbilical outstretch normal human indents, their tummies are lopsided and atypical.

Finally, at home, our hired *watchiman* accompanies me out on our porch as a day's-end breeze enwraps us while a pot of pinto beans cooks and we patiently await for our *stay* to uplift.

We tuned to our late-night newscasts, some reporters inform of our parole's continuance tomorrow. Its extension will remain strict and for us to comply with their military and bureaucratic commands. A newscaster interviewed a political analyst and both agreed on our drama, "We're imprisoned in our own houses." True, whatever happened to Hondurans' translucency? I do not know, and our crisis response teams do not reveal any details of its cause or anticipate an end date.

One only needs to discern our various newscasts—our only informants—channel 7's broadcasts are about how our two principal civic figures disagree on social and political issues and, because of this drastic contrast of their political agendas, neither wants to give up this lucrative throne. Channel 2 maintains a bluish flashy carousel of forthcoming programs every day, our redundant guide to nowhere; that is, 162 paid-for channels yet no new shows to watch. Remarkably, channel 5 airs that our principal politician *was coup'd* out of his power-seat by a covert military exertion and its successor *is* in power by way of those same militants. Are lunatics in psychiatry wards and prisons only? *Hum.*

Our future now in jeopardy makes one think of when will

this *state-of-surge* conclude, and why our average citizen has to withstand *their* controversial consequences? Furthermore, energized citizens are ready to summon independent radio and T.V. Medias to voice their opinions, concerns, and sorrows that have resulted from this unfortunate split of forces deadlock and, indeed, no average citizen has received a nickel to stay home and everyone must eat. Tomorrow will be our third day and ever-ready angry shopkeepers coupled with our general populace will head for our streets to propagate democracy, within our permitted timeframe, and to demonstrate to our apparent inept regime of our educative motor, financial matrix, and product losses. Our swift breach to commercial self-sufficiency.

Will we move into civil unrest? I do not know—anyhow, they also put out a statewide ban to liquor businesses and that is not cool. *Ley Seca: Dry Law.* Not when our beers' national name here is *Salva Vida,* Life-Saver. A counterpoise befalls me as a desperate gulp of a cold one has increased whereas, meanwhile, our cardinal at our local cathedral is the first to get *his* shot-glass of sanctified lifesaver every morning, afternoon, and evening mass. He does not appear dehydrated or succumbed to our dryness, or its law.

Of course, some vendors ignore it and go underground but risk arrest and a bunch of bureaucratic red-tape problems for a prompt bail, if captured. Therefore, our quest for these isolated poor salespeople is enigmatic. A contradictory belief here is that an overwhelmed majority of our populace is unarmed so it is in our best interest to stay calm and patient for a much-needed resolve to this unnerving power plight. While relaxed in front of our set-top boxes, we listen to their lashings—as our channels main attraction is yellow journalism and fear-inductive propaganda, it has become repetitive and weary, as tomorrow, a follow-up marathon of political dysfunction awaits us.

All be it, every time a gubernatorial representative prepares a public message, radio and visual Medias spotlight such a person, and this appears as though our legislators monopolize our intercommunicative signals without alternate views or practical answers in sight.

Never in my smoky adventures anticipated or construed to live chastised. Perhaps my oft-jailed life is a heaven sent cue of our ultimate paradise and not a purgatory fairy-tale as some have me believe. My hometown, a free man's land, yet am not. Probably, no person is sovereign in this life span, it sounds shameful and scary. No one is truly safe or free from statecraft scrutiny.

Between heaven and earth, some angels say, not a fart remains hidden anymore, only egocentric men that obstruct peoples' constitutional rights. My hay awaits.

HOME ALONE

"Men are not prisoners of fate, but only prisoners of their own minds."—*Franklin D. Roosevelt (1882-1945)*

Our republics' mandated home arrest is not popping-up any *piñatas* or confetti candidly. *Rats!* They are not even propelling our customary premier series to view and its chaotic state is evoking harsh patterns of helplessness, anxiety, and depression because we are without straight-to-the-point updates about what *really* happened with this military coup. Our visual networks run infomercials throughout our day and radio antennas, music. After 10:00 P.M., we have a handful of programs to watch due to "technical issues". This political melodrama makes one think of a possible supreme puppeteer group that suddenly has directed our tracks and my mistrust is that our *pay-per-view* satellite is carefully blocked—as its newscasts is one-sided.

In addition, any time that our predetermined programs unexpectedly return, its overall televised content is a modified mixture of Mexican and South-American episodes. We are bored of rerun shows over-and-again, plus, its regulated structure makes it appear as though we are under subjective communism with an applied monitor-ship of our view preferences.

My neighbors said that of our normal tasks' freeze is in effect from 10 A.M. to 6 P.M. Our time now is 9:00 A.M. and, just as time passes by, so too merchants walk slowly onto our streets although no public official, on any Media, has confirmed or endorsed any proposal for anyone to exit our houses so far. These early birds probably get a head start to run errands or head to their regular jobs and to beat an early morning jam.

Our set-top box came alive at 8:00 A.M. and quickly tuned various channels, and because within our curfew timeframe, only our Honduran flag is in display on our monitor's screen. As we skim its newsreel to see if we may go anywhere, one of its reporters said that we must *stay* tune for a very important message from our country's *Republic,* its legislators, who up to this sequence is an interim president, however, so far, nothing. *Another gag order?*

As of now, house chores keep me in a flow of thoughts and acts so as not to anguish about our domestic freeze. Amongst homely activities that keep me busy is another prison tactic to hand-wash the lone outfit I wore when exiled, which is, a boxer short and blue jeans, a tee shirt and tennis shoes. Besides, when anyone of authority establishes a timeframe for any person to exit and re-enter a certain property, as if by approval only, is a curfew—a known form of dictatorship.

Anyhow, my white tennis shoes have turned brown from my long walks through the dusty cane fields and dirt streets that these same political leaders always guarantee to pave even without setting datelines. Like rapper M.C. Breed sings, "Ain't no future in yo frontin." Yow! Empty raps.

A *siesta* habit every afternoon overpasses my conscious strength, which, nevertheless, it makes me feel more relaxed and re-energized for our day's evening. In contrast, is a lack of my daily thoughtfulness as this is not healthy, it is of great conscious help under our peculiar contingencies.

Oh yes, *our coup,* they have soft-soaped us as our journalism agencies only develop inconsistent and confused chaff and, to our dismay, interrupt our regular net-flicks with frequent hyped-up false news alarms. Every time every channel unexpectedly switches to its prime signal provider—that appears to belong to a rich person or group, we know an important politician will make an across-our-board brief. Afterwards, at every blockage, mostly everyone halts whatever we were involved in just to listen in on his or her messages so as not to remain ignorant and taken to the slammer. Any gubernatorial mandate that trickles down to our public gets a hasty relay as they utilize every media resource under their command.

Furthermore, after any "live" political fuss, our broadcast provider relieves its audience with this message, "You may now continue viewing your favorite programming." Twenty-first century visual, verbal, and cerebral manipulative devices. Today's *home detainees,* tomorrow's *home prisoners.* A deep contemplative prayer and a nap will decompress me.

Another night passes away although an aura of sickness overpowers me—but not of politics, well, yeah, that too. A haphazard cold or flu has me with a sore throat due to, I think, our weather's drastic changes and my lean body has not adapted to it, yet; or from swallowing our streets' dust, probably. That is, one minute our atmosphere is fiery and suddenly it rains with lightning strikes that illuminate our heavens and makes our expansive black sky sound wrathful, wild and almost scary, for an adult. When it rains, it does not produce coolness; it just makes our heat lower one or two degrees yet its humidity skyrockets.

For example, today it was dark, cloudy—and breezy. I liked it. Sometimes our dark skies dispenses briskly rains that refreshes our atmosphere and body temperatures a bit. Anyhow, it is 9:00 P.M., I am tired, drained, and cannot concentrate on any one particular project, theme, idea or goal to pursue—*hell! Gunshots!—Gunshots! Shhh. Outside of our house. I am ducking!* Five or six nearby pistol bangs. An absolute clear and dramatic explosion of bullets that echoed inside of our empty house and those were not firecrackers.

As quick as those blasts ignited I prompted to turn our lights off, lurked and peeped outside to survey our adjacent houses, being thankful of our streets' bright lights. No one was outside, it was no drive-by shootout, we are not at war and it is not Christmas. Anyhow, kept my eyes wide open and ears doggedly attentive on what occurred outside, as it is critical because those bullets blasted excessively close to home. Moreover, someone whom I cannot see has a loaded pistol and is not afraid to pull its trigger.

———

My third day in Honduras and alone in my home country, without basic social support from anyone here, and not even an identity card to present myself as who I say I am. An extreme contrast from prison life where everyone must have an identification from his or her first day. Furthermore, a quick flash is that people do not make a favor without a refund of some sort—so if my symptoms go beyond a simple sinus, who will help me with the run-arounds? As it is, at my forefront is a dragged citizenship process. It is comprehensive logic as an unpronounced belief here is not what one can do for this country whereas what this country cannot do for one. An instinct is that everyone has noticed my strong fluid Mexican-American accent, lack of Spanish derogatory words and keep-the-wheels-turning manners, and with it, follows an apprehensive prejudice. An unasked facial tilted look of, "Are you certain of where you just arrived?"

As my familiarization unfolds, it is okay that this trek will be a scrupulous experience to google honest Hondurans with similar interests. For instance, one objective would be to start a basketball or baseball team; in contrast, our overwhelmed populace here are soccer fanatics. Cultural differences that will take some time to modify, for example, to carry a weapon at all times whether registered, or not. *Hangman, anyone?*

What is happening to our country? *Okay.* So far, we are aware that we have had too many days of usurp regime changes, though this does not mean to put us on furlough as they may take care of their political matters behind closed doors. Where is our democracy? Does democracy even exist here? Is democracy in Honduras the same as in configurative democratic republics?

Albeit, most verbal political warnings come via televised and boom-box frequencies mainly as a reminder for us to remain indoors until official pre-ordained notice—though more often at its precise draft and, as a result to this disarray, everyone's favorite quote is, "Oh, that's how it is here in Honduras."

Withal, our logic is to abide under its Laws and not risk an arrest for disregard of it. In short, our parliament's venom is still pungent as both disgruntled parties lash out at themselves, therefore, more *Seasaw* days ahead. An unfortunate conditional aftermath for political nonparticipants, honest business committed citizens and middle class as it affects our everyday responsibilities. Settling in this country is tougher than Clearway Correctional Authorities' ways; and to adjust even risky. Whereas, every time a *coup* continues, everyone loses money, as we cannot go out and search for a way to earn our day's food as both of our major feuding political parties are not refunding a penny to anyone.

Anyhow, earlier today and after a presidential mobility grant with perimeters, rode my bicycle through the *cañeras* and just before exiting a sloped ditch, laid the bicycle, and in front of me zigzagged a coiled ropey yellow-and-black striped snake with its erect head rapidly stretching into about half-a-meter lengthwise. Like a Popsicle, leaned and stared at it—so as not to lose sight of it, and out of nowhere, a green gecko sprinted past my feet and the snake picked-up chase. *Pfew!*

This encounter with wild reptiles scared my crap out. That snake could have easily bitten me before it targeted that lizard. It will probably not catch that tiny speedy reptile as it did a "poof" act into the bushes. Now, an extra awareness is necessary whenever entering those sugarcane fields' dirt canal. Every time it pours suddenly, it turns this dirt road into a muddy saturation making it difficult to stride it, and cycling impossible. That doughy slime makes whomever passes through get off their bicycles and continue by foot for its clay accumulation on our tennis shoes makes our thighs and lower backs exhaust faster.

On our extreme side, this country's crime spree over here must be at a horrific appraisal for its indicative is that mostly everywhere in San Pedro Sula, the majority of locals share stories of recent robberies and murders as if describing an ice-cream purchase. Thereupon, our Medias' attractiveness is violent crime, gangs, guns and drug traffic: terror. This lifestyle has begun to have a negative impact on my psyche and it ingrains an absolute sense of fear, vulnerability, and strict precautionary assessments are past due. Top of my to-do list, to purchase a handgun, a rifle, an Uzi, a grenade or a rocket-launcher.

Not that every man here is up to no good, but results are an apprehensiveness of our ever-present criminal underpinnings. For example, this evening while walking around our block that leads to a friendly bakery when suddenly a public *rapidito* swooped beside me, obstructing my path, its two occupants got off and asked if I had a journey in mind and, if so, they would take care of it at half-price. As they pinpointed stared me down, I replied a shaky "no"—nervous because these mini-buses are not to circulate inside of our gated residency. Somehow, they *talked* their way into our residency, bypassed our security guards, and now only search for clients even though it is past six p.m. and every nine-to-fiver gallops into their homes as major streets are deserted.

In retrospect, its driver and his assistant did not appear to be genuinely in search of passengers, rather, victims.

Furthermore, this is not their travel route, as most residents in here have their own vehicles.

Social insecurity and political turmoil, our day and night extreme heats with heavy unexpected downpours are having some degree of negative impact on my attitude and require immediate changes at once. That is, perhaps a return to enriching activities such as deep-breathing, ruminate and positive thought buildup so as to not go berserk with this madness around me at once—and beyond these experiences, *our coup.* A refreshingly cold beer to ease my nerves, which ache to fleet our chaos, then to hibernate.

ANALYSIS OF A HOMIE

Nightmarish. Three bedroom-size pitch-black dungeons; two on our left side of a long obscure entryway. Inside of this cage and to its right, at a roof-high corner, is a tiny two-bar aperture with a wispy streak of streetlight penetrating a scanty distribution to, at the very least, contour roughly ten bodies standing next to each other. On its floor, it felt like debris lying about: empty recyclable water and beverage bottles, plastic forks and spoons, crushed Styrofoam plates and cups.

Our light's flicker is hardly visible and only sufficient to draw out a couple of malevolent faces. As we moved, one sensed trashed objects lied about such as empty grocery bags, cigarette boxes, and pieces of aluminum foils and toward its middle, a strong smell of drain-water accompanied by accumulated urine from every man held for public drunkenness and heinous criminal offenses.

Everyone tried to sit, lay, or crouch by its barred door, as it was our only waterless space with a tiny bit of cold wind rushing in. Ever so slowly, throughout this night and subconsciously, we rotated so that everyone may get some fresh air while two or three got a chance to sit on a tiny dry area. We needed to be extra careful and not walk on this cell's complete dark side for a risk to step on excrement hereby increase its already present awful putrid stench combined with stagnant rainwater. No toilettes, faucets, showers or any flow of water anywhere; just one black ancient unit.

An isolated yet distinct gulag with one police guard entering intermittently with another drunk or homicidal. Everyone looked sleepy for not catching zees because of not enough dry space to lay down in its tightness. Their faces were hard pictures of young and old, meek and distrustful faces of Hispanics and Blacks. Thankfully, on this night of tropical downpour, no larvae, mosquitoes, flies or insects, and rats or mice; heretofore, a miracle.

A moment to move arrived and my second turn to sit on its floor and quickly dozed-off but slept in instability with my head wobbled and my neck and upper back stiff as it hurt, hence, my mobility handicapped. A few times, my eyes would blink just to see who the new man in our cell was and instantly pass out again.

At a certain time, we did not fit and we hoped that no one else arrived for that would push us further into its voided middle as no one could see what laid in there. No one said a word, only comprehensively inched along its clay brick walls.

A cell next to us was parallel, therefore, not visible; however, at our hallway's end another steely barred door was visible with its reflective shadow. And in it, two or three times a lone man approached *it* to grip its crossbars and only his wrinkled aged face became somewhat decipherable. He was an abandoned soul. On this eternal night, our prison remained mostly quiet with someone's occasional abrupt delirious scream, "Let me out of here! I didn't do anything!"

An electrical thunderstorm poured and dissipated but left our atmosphere hot, humid and sticky yet bearable wilderness temperature.

A natural light arose and its scenery of bright rays slowly began to penetrate through our heightened cranny cavity—it enlivened our cell and resuscitated bodies. It anticipated our desperate wills of any outside bodily operations as it introduced guards, civilians, notary publics and attorneys—poor souls dedicated to perform business on a church's brilliant day and spectacular cloud-free sunrise. Young and old women carried toddlers and baskets full of warm corn tortillas and flour *baleadas* filled with refried beans and sold those meals accompanied with either hot homegrown coffee or chocolate. Amidst our bustle of decent hard-at-work salespersons, our daytime guard responsible for this prison's keys said out loud and threatened, "No one is getting out until six this evening—so don't ask me what time of day it is!"

> "There are two good things in life, freedom
> of thought and freedom of action."
> —*W. Somerset Maugham (1874-1965)*[iii]

EPILOGUE

Thank you so much for your patience. *Ahhhh.*

A few seconds more so as not to hold you much longer, here are some quick loose notes to this long unplanned journey. That is, Corky, a stray bullet struck and killed him in a non-gang, non-drive-by, non-drug related incident inside of a discotheque gunfire in 1990, at age 20, while the rest of us served time. He never knew jail or cited for any infractions in his lifetime. Pugs, was deported to Guatemala in 1991 and stabbed to death days after his arrival when he would not release his wallet to a band of crooks; he was 21. Peelainsky was ambushed in a resisting arrest police shoot-out in 2008, he was 34 years of age.

I know not Camus, Hemingway, or Stephen King, but I know experiences.

The End.

The Man's Office

The Homie's Office

CONCLUSION

Statistics relating to crime, captivity, culprits and recidivism overwhelm us and, at times, are bored and confused. Numbers are not of my preference, numbers do not cheat, people do; however, alchemy is in numbers. A glance at our Federal Bureau of Justice 2001 Statistics about Jail Re-entry Trends says that from its top 16 counties in the United States with highest incarcerations of persons, 10 of those counties are in Califas.

The Office of Juvenile Justice and Delinquency Prevention statistics show that on a typical day in 2017, about 3,600 persons under 18 years of age were inmates in U.S. adult jails and by year's end, almost 1,000 were in adult state prison custody.

A Second Chance Act of 2007[iv] report reveals that annually approximately 650,000 convicts came out of state and federal prisons and between 10 and 12 million more were set free from local jails. Additionally, those freed persons struggle with drug abuse, inadequate education and proper job skills, ego issues and lack of counselors, and a large number of those conditioned releases return to prison within three years due to, partly, unsuited social programs and opportunities. Nearly 432,000 of those inmates exiting penitentiary institutions will probably commit a new felony or serious misdemeanor conviction within three years of their commutes. Such high backslide rates equal thousands of new crimes each year.

Once, a Los Diablos County Probation Officer kindly said to me, "Go into your pain, absorb it, hold it, analyze it, confront it and dissolve it, holistic and without using alcohol or drugs and you will rediscover your true self." Homie, whatever prison you are in, *just try* to take heed of his advice.

Finally, every phase of our homie's eccentric runarounds are infusing collectively—of age, like a pungent Roquefort, and making sense—a million thanks to various probation officers who advised me to always observe our laws' right side—Alex Garcia, 2020.

Made in Prison / Hecho en Prisión / Free our Homie

ENDNOTES

All quotations marked with an asterisk (*) are from "The Macmillan Dictionary of Quotations", Chartwell Books Inc. (2002) Edison, New Jersey; U.S.A.

i   https://www.wisefamousquotes.com/nelson-mandela-quotes/2009; Last accessed October 3, 2019
ii Master Chen Yen, Contemplative Outreach Pamphlet, *n.d/n.p* Circa 2010
iii https://www.The FreeDictionaryword.of.the.day@farlex.com; Last accessed November 14, 2019
iv https://en.wikipedia.org/Second Chance Act 2007; Last accessed December 31, 2019

Printed in the United States
By Bookmasters